Maksym Kolomyjec

Tanks in the Winter war
1939-1940

Translation: Tim Dinan

Leandoer & Ekholm Publishing, Stockholm
2009

Original title: Pansar i vinterkriget 1939-1940
Writer: Maksym Kolomyjec
Maps: Samuel Svärd
Translation: Tim Dinan
Original copyright: Leandoer & Ekholm Förlag 2006
Illustrations: Arkadiusz Wrobel, Andriej Aksenov, Grzergorz Jackowski, Maarten Swarts
Layout: Daniel Åberg/Åberg stilus et forma
Leandoer & Ekholm förlag HB, Stockholm
www.leforlag.se
Copyright© Leandoer & Ekholm Förlag, Stockholm 2011
Second edition, 2011

Printed at: Spaustuve Spindulys, Kaunas, Litauen, 2011
ISBN. 978-91-975895-2-9
Cover: A column of T-28's from the 20th Heavy Tank Battalion on the move, Karelian Isthmus, Feb. 1940. (RGAKFD)
Picture sources: RGAKFD, Ryssland; ASKM, Ryssland; RIGVA, Ryssland; IWM, England
TM Bovington, England; Esa Muikku, Finland; I. Periyaslavtcev, Ryssland; Leandoer & Ekholm Arkiv
Photos with no source given in the caption, all originate from Leandoer & Ekholm archives.
According to Swedish and EC laws, the publisher is considered the only rightful owner of the contents in this publication.

All rights reserved. No part of this publication may be reproduced, stored in a retrieval system, or transmitted, in any form or by any means, electronic, mechanical, photocopying, recording or otherwise, without the prior permission of the publisher and copyright holder.

Table of contents

1: • Background
1:1 • Introduction 7
1:2 • The conflict's history 11

2: • The beginning of the conflict
2:1 • The war begins 17
2:2 • Tank forces of the USSR and Finland 31

3: • Battles
3:1 • Battles on the Karelian isthmu 59
3:2 • Tank forces in battle on the Karelian isthmus 87
3:3 • Battles north of Ladoga 117
3:4 • Battles in the 9th army sector 131
3:5 • The fights in the Murmansk sector 147
3:6 • Home production for the front 153

4: • Appendix
4:1 • Tank personnel who received the commendation "Hero of the Soviet Union" for their contribution in the Soviet-Finnish War 160
4:2 • Vehicle facts appendix with pictures 165
4:3 • Literature and sources 175
4:4 • Maps and tank illustrations 177
4:5 • Blueprints 209

Background

A motorcyclist leaves off a battle report to the crew of a BA-10 armoured car on the Karelian Isthmus, 1939. "Overall" type mud-feet have been installed on the tank's back-wheels to increase traction in the snow. (RGAKFD)

A captured Finnish Vickers that was tested on the Kubinka proving grounds (outside of Moscow) spring of 1940. On the photo, the mounting plate for a Suomi 9-mm-submachinegun can be seen on the tank's front. (RGVA)

1.1 Introduction

Until just recently, studies of the Soviet-Finnish War (or, as it is called in the West, "The Winter War") that took place between November 30, 1939 and March 13, 1940, have primarily been confined to a few Russian historians. A relatively large number of publications on this subject have come out only in the last few years. Moreover, most of these contributions deal with the conflict's political aspects and the war's overall course, without devoting much attention to the role played by specific weapons and the combat units formed around them..

This writing is entirely devoted to the performance of the tank forces that took part in the Winter War. It's based on many years of archive research and studies of both Soviet and Finnish documents. In our opinion, we can therefore give an objective picture of the roll played by tanks in this conflict. Nevertheless, our work does not claim to completely exhaust all the information on this subject: Many questions remain unanswered where we haven't been able to unearth relevant archive material. The author is therefore very thankful for any and all comments, or additional information addressed to M V Kolomits, Box 373, 121096 Moscow.

The author expressly wishes to thank M. Svirin, the co-workers at the War Powers Central Museum – N. Lavrenko. O.Tolstovaja, and E. Gmyr – as well as, N. Gavrilkin, M. Makaov, L. Vachin and his Finnish colleague, Esa Muikku, for the help they have given me in writing this account.

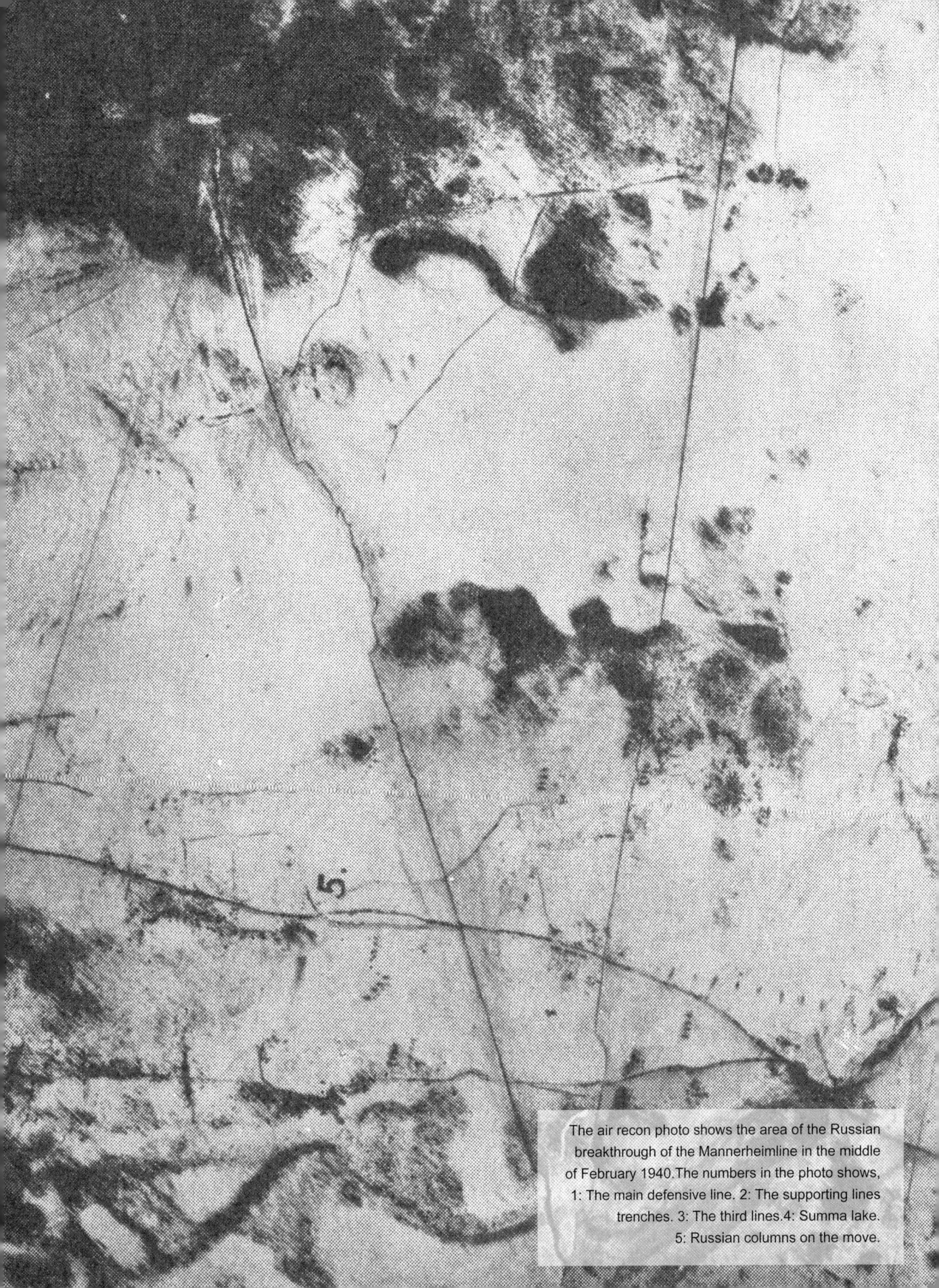

The air recon photo shows the area of the Russian breakthrough of the Mannerheimline in the middle of February 1940. The numbers in the photo shows, 1: The main defensive line. 2: The supporting lines trenches. 3: The third lines. 4: Summa lake. 5: Russian columns on the move.

Preparing for battle: a type Sokolov sled holding infantry soldiers being towed by a SHT-130 tank. The rounded tops of the flamethrower fueltanks can be seen to the left of the tank's turret, the Northwest Front, Jan. 1940. (CAFM)

1:2 The conflict's history

Finland is one of the countries that succeeded in gaining its independence as a result of the revolution in Russia. But even before this revolution, Finland had been autonomous: As the Grand Duchy of Finland within the Russian Empire, it had its own self-governing political body. On December 18, 1917, the Soviet Union recognized the nation of Finland as being fully independent. However, the relationship between the two countries became marred by complications that arose during the period that followed.

On August 23, 1939, Germany and the Soviet Union signed a non-aggression treaty. Also undersigned within the parameters of this treaty was an appended secret protocol, or clause, known as the "Molotov-Ribbentrop Pact," in which the USSR and Germany apportioned their respective spheres of influence in Europe. According to this protocol, Lithuania, Latvia, Estonia and Finland fell under the Soviet Union's sphere of influence

On September 1, 1939, Germany launched its attack against Poland. The Second World War began. On the 17th of September, the Soviet Union likewise initiated preparations for launching a war with the declared intent of freeing those territories in the West Ukraine and western Belarus that belonged to Poland, but had previously been a part of Russia.

Between September 28 and October 10, 1939, the Soviet Union, in accord with the appended protocol, negotiated military treaties establishing mutual defence with Latvia, Lithuania and Estonia. As a condition of these treaties, the USSR was permitted to station troops and establish military bases inside the territories of these countries. Only 8 days later, on October 18, units from the Red Army were already moving into the territories of these Baltic nations.

On October 5, Finland received a USSR proposal that it enter a mutual defence agreement. But the Finish government had no intention of signing such a disadvantageous treaty. Consequently, on October 6, Finland called up its military reservists and began mobilizing its armed forces.

On October 12, negotiations were begun in Moscow between the government of the Soviet Union and representatives of the Finnish government. The Soviet leadership had taken great pains to prepare for these negotiations. They had drawn up two treaty variations aimed at winning Finland's agreement to give up the eastern section of the Karelian Isthmus, a few islands in the Gulf of Finland, and parts of the of the Rybatjij peninsula to the Soviet Union. In addition, the Soviet Union sought the right to build a military base on the Hanko peninsula. In compensation, Finland would receive territory in East Karelia twice the size of the land area it would be giving up. The USSR's strategic need of the Hanko peninsula was motivated by the Red Army's possession of analogous bases in Estonia. If the Soviet Union got the right to use the Hanko peninsula, artillery emplacements could then fully cover the entrance to the Gulf of Finland. A concurrent aim of the Soviet government was to further protect the security of Leningrad by moving the USSR/Finnish border on the Karelian isthmus approximately 80 kilometers to the north (At that time, Leningrad's suburbs lay only 32 km from the Finnish border). Individual members of the Finnish government's leadership had widely divergent views about the Soviet Union's proposal. The country's president, J.K. Passikivi, and Field Marshall G. Mannaheim held that the territorial concessions were acceptable, while the Finance Minister, V. Tanner, and Foreign Minister, E. Erkko, held the opposite. In the end, it was decided that only limited concessions could be made: a shift of the border on the Karelian Isthmus of 10-20 km. and an exchange of four islands in the Gulf of Finland in return for territory in East Karelia. As far as the leasing of Hanko peninsula, the answer was no.

At the negotiations held in Moscow over September 23-25 and November 2-4, a successful compromise could not be reached, despite J. Stalin's willingness to accept a series of concessions. Among other things, he was prepared to have the border on the Karelian Isthmus moved only 40 km, instead of 80: "Inasmuch as Leningrad cannot be moved, we ask that the border be drawn at a distance of 70 km. from Leningrad: We are asking for 2 700 square kilometers and offering 5 500 square kilometers in exchange."

The main stumbling-block in the negotiations was Finland's unwillingness to lease the Hanko peninsula – alternatively, one of the near-by islands. The Soviet leadership regarded this as the most vital point in the negotiations. And without an agreement on this point having been reached, the negotiations ground to a halt.

As early as the second half of October, when it was clear that reaching some agreement with Finland was hardly likely, the combat readiness level of Leningrad's Military District (LVO), and in the naval fleets of the North and Baltic Seas, was raised. On October 29, LVO's staff submitted an "Operation plan for crushing the Finnish military's land and sea war-capability" to the USSR's Minister of Defence. On October 15, the LVO staff had been ordered to complete a troop-summation by November 20. It required less than a week to carry out the enormous task of preparing the various military units for an attack, while, at the same time, in the Red Army's general headquarters there weren't even maps covering the terrain of the area they planned to attack.

According to this plan, the strategic thinking was to crush Finland's military defences within the course of two-three weeks by launching a massive strike with similarly massive military forces. Stalin approved this, while the General Chief of Staff, Sjaposjnikov, to the contrary, considered that engaging war against Finland, "… is not a simple mission, but will require at least several months of intensive and demanding battles." Apparently, it was

A T-26, model 1933 (with a ring-formed antenna around the turret, a P-40 anti-aircraft machine gun, and a spot light for night combat) from the 100th Tank Battalion rolling towards battle in the 8th Army Zone, Dec. 1939. (CAFM)

for this reason that Sjaposjnikov was sent to the Back Sea on long vacation.

On November 26, 1939, an incident took place on the Karelian Isthmus that later became known as the "Shelling of Mainila." According to a news report issued by TASS, on this day, at 3:45 pm, the Finnish artillery had shelled a location near the border outside the village of Mainila, causing the death of four Red Army personnel and nine wounded. Some few hours later, V. Molotov delivered a note to the Finnish ambassador in the USSR, wherein the events in Mainila were characterized as an "enemy aggression against the USSR." In connection with this incident, Finland was advised to draw its army back 20-25 km from the border. In its responding note, the Finnish government stated its supposition that perhaps the incident in Mainila was possibly the result of artillery practice from the Soviet side, and consequently suggested the creation of a mutual commission to investigate the events in question. It was further suggested in this note that both the Finnish and the Soviet troops should be withdrawn from the border.

The Finnish government's answer produced a very negative reaction from the USSR's leadership. In its response, issued on the November 28, Moscow stated that Finland's unchanged position meant that the country will "… keep Leningrad under threat" and "drive the upcoming crisis to its farthest extreme." And finally, it made clear that the Soviet Union herewith annulled the non-aggression pact between the USSR and Finland of 1932. The following day, November 29, in a note from Molotov, the Finnish ambassador was informed that the attack against the Soviet border units had continued, and consequently the Soviet government was not in a position "to uphold normal ties with Finland, but was forced to call home its political and economic representatives from Finland." This clearly indicated a complete break between the USSR and Finland. Not even a message from the Finnish government, received in Moscow on that very same day, stating that it was willing to unilaterally withdraw its troops from the border was able to deflect the course of events. On the morning of November 30, 1939, the Soviet weapons began to speak. The Winter War began.

The beginning of the conflict

T-26 tanks and "Komsomolets" artillery tractors en route to an assault. 8th Army Zone, Dec, 2 1939. . (CAFM)

A type T-26 tank, model 1933 (with a ring, rail-like antenna around the turret, a P-40 anti-aircraft machine gun, and a spot light for night combat) from the 39th Light Tank Brigade on watch, Karelian Isthmus, Jan 1940 (RGAKFD)

2:1 The war begins

On the morning of November 30, at 8:30 a.m., following preliminary artillery bombardment, the Red Army crossed the border into Finland, extending from the Gulf of Finland to the White Sea. Altogether, 21 infantry divisions from Leningrad's military district were set in along the 1,610 kilometer border. On the Karelian Isthmus, the 7th Army (nine infantry divisions, a tank corps, and three tank brigades) advanced towards Petrozavodsk. In central Karela, the 8th Army (six rifle divisions, and a tank brigade) advanced towards Kandalaksja, Uchta and Reboly, and the 14th Army (three rifle divisions) advanced towards Murmansk All told, the forces assembled for the invasion of Finland numbered some 400 000 men, 1,476 combat tanks, 1,915 artillery pieces, and approximately 1,000 airplanes. The army's operations were supported by border soldiers, NKVD-units, and by the respective naval fleets of the Baltic Sea and Artic Ocean.

Direct responsibility for the preparation and execution of battle operations fell on the shoulders of Major General K. Mereskov, commander of Leningrad's Military District; A. Zjdanov, a member of the military council; and on chief of staff, Major General I. Smorodinov. In addition, a general staff was formed in Moscow under the leadership of K Vorosjilov, which included: J. Stalin, B. Sjaposjnikov, and N. Kuznetsov (people's commissioner of the USSR's navy).

The Finnish army began to mobilize in October of 1939, and by the outbreak of the war had ten rifle divisions, four infantry brigades, one infantry regiment, 31 infantry battalions and one cavalry brigade. In addition, behind the front, two more infantry divisions made up of reservists were formed. On the Karelian Isthmus, the Isthmus Army was assigned six infantry divisions and National Guard forces. Two infantry divisions were located in the Petrozavodsk area. North of them, on up to the Artic Ocean, there were only individual regiments and battalions, along with military border patrol units.

In all, the army consisted of 265,000 men, 534 artillery pieces (excluding coast artillery), 64 combat tanks

A Finnish soldier tries out a armored shield made by the Russians.

A machinegun bunker in the Mannerheim line in November 1939. Thanks to snow, it is impossible to see it until it´s crew opens fi re wth the machineguns.

Finish soldiers constructing a bunker on the Karelian Isthmus summer 1940.

T-26 tanks (models 1939 and 1933) along with GAZ-M1 and GAZ-AA cars on their way to the Karelian Isthmus front, Dec. 1939. (CAFM)

and 270 airplanes. In addition, there were approximately 500,000 people within Finland's borders who had some form of military training.

Leading the overall war effort was a general staff formed under the command of Field Marshal Gustav Mannerheim.

Finland's anti-tank defences

The entire area, from the old Soviet-Finnish border to Vyborg was covered by vast, heavily wooded forests that only permitted tanks to move along roadways and occasional openings in the woods. A large number of rivers and lakes with swamp-like and/or steeply inclined shorelines, numerous deep ravines, marshy peat-bogs that never froze, and large blocks of stone - all these terrain features formed a natural, almost insurmountable barrier to tanks. The ability of tank units to carry out maneuvers was made even worse by a notable lack of roads and progress through barely passable belts of forest required great skill on the part of drivers forced to maneuver between trees and blocks of stone.

Moreover, the hard winter of 1939-40 with bitter cold (minus 45-49 degrees centigrade in January 1940) and deep snow cover (90-120 cm) added further difficulties to the deployment of tanks.

The Mannerheim line

Complementing the natural obstacles on the Karelian Isthmus was the Finnish defence system, which is denoted as "The Mannerheim Line" (after Marshal C. Mannerheim) in our reading of in-country literature. Reference to this line encompassed the entire system of permanent installations and obstacles constructed on the Karelian Isthmus that reportedly stretched to a length of 135 km and a breadth of up to 90 km. Essentially, it comprised a security zone – the main defence line and a second, rear-defence line – plus the defence lines protecting Vyborg and a series of freestanding positions at the most threatened sectors. In Finnish literature it is understood that "the Mannerheim Line" invariably refers to the defence line where the Red Army's offensive was actually halted in December 1939. This borderline does not entirely coincide with the officially designated main line of defence (agreement was up to approximately 70 percent). Therefore many military historians in the West distinguish between the Finnish concept "The Mannerheim Line" and "the system of Finnish fortifications on the Karelian Isthmus." In this record, for the sake of simplicity, we will be referring to the entire system of fortifications on the Karelian Isthmus as "The Mannerheim Line."

The construction of fortifications on the Karelian Isthmus began as early as the fall of 1918. However, the construction of a more comprehensive plan for the defence of the Karelian Isthmus was carried out during the years 1920-24, under the leadership of Major General O. Enckell, the general chief of staff of Finland's Armed Forces. During these five years of construction, the fortifications so emplaced (in certain references known as "Enckell's defence emplacements") later became the central defence-zone in "The Mannerheim Line." It consisted of 18 central defence points, each comprised of field fortifications (redoubts) of lumber and earth (ry. DZOT), permanent stone and concrete bunkers (ry. DOT), along with anti-tank and infantry obstacles. In all, during the years 1920-24, 168 concrete installations were constructed in connection with "Enckell's defence emplacements." Further construction of "The Mannerheim Line" was again taken up in 1932 and continued until the start of the Winter War. The work was led by the well-known Finnish fortification expert, Colonel I Fabricius. During this time the security zone, the secondary and rear defence zones, as well as the defence-line protecting Vyborg were established. At certain particularly susceptible sectors, new separate emplacements were created. On the central defence line old bunkers were modernized and complemented with bunkers of a new type. These came to be called "millions-bunkers" because of their high cost – millions of Finnish marks were spent on their construction. "Millions-bunkers" had two to three battlefield barracks connected by underground passageways. Even these tunnels fulfilled the role of barracks, as 20 to 60 men could seek shelter inside them. All installations had their own provisions (water, electricity, heat, supply of foodstuffs and ammunition), which made it possible for the individual garrisons to maintain an effective defence even under a full blockade. The walls of the battlefield barracks had a thickness of 130-150 cm, reinforced with 4-7 armored plates with an average thickness of 280-490 mm. The bunkers were covered with a

A trophy captured by the Red Army shown in the "Crushing of the White-Finns" exhibition in Leningrad, Mar, 1940; A Renault type FT-17 tank. (ASKM)

Finlands only modern tank before 1940 were the Brittish-made Vickers. It was armed with a 37mm gun. Here one can see the short-barrelled version. Shortly before the outbreak of the war, it was replaced by a long-barrelled version.

A anti-tank line is being built: Granite blocks arranged in lines will be reinforced with concrete.

Two meter high, reinforced concrete anti-tank obstacle, Karelian Isthmus, Dec, 1939

3.5-4.5 meter thick layer of sand and stone. In order to better view the battlefield, the "millions-bunkers" were equipped with several small observation towers, covered with 160-180 mm armored plate.

The battlefield barracks' armament consisted of several machine guns of the "maxim-type" (single barrelled machine guns) and during the course of the war, the effectiveness of some bunkers was strengthened by the addition of 37 mm Bofors cannons and armored vehicle rifles. In the interest of fairness, it should be pointed out that total number of "millions-bunkers" was not large and that they were built at the most sensitive sectors. In all, along the central defence line at the start of the war there were 210 bunkers (DOT) and 546 lumber-and-earth defence installations (DZOT). An additional 26 bunkers and 61 lumber-and-earth emplacements were constructed along the rear defence line and locations in the Vyborg area.

Bunkers and lumber-and-earth emplacements were tactically united to form defence-centers held together by a well thought out system of firing positions for artillery, machine guns and grenade launchers. The field troops were positioned between permanent installations – in rifle trenches, connecting passageways, and central firing locations that were often shielded by armored plate and concrete. All installations on "The Mannerheim Line"

An anti-tank escarpment in the Mannerheim Line, Feb. 1940. (CAFM)

A timber anti-tank barrier, Karelian Isthmus, Feb. 1940. (CAFM)

Six rows of granite stone anti-tank obstacles – typical of the Mannerheim Line. (CAFM)

Various barbed wire and timber obstacles, Karelian Isthmus, Jan. 1940. (CAFM)

An anti-tank escarpment in the Mannerheim Line, Feb. 1940. (CAFM)

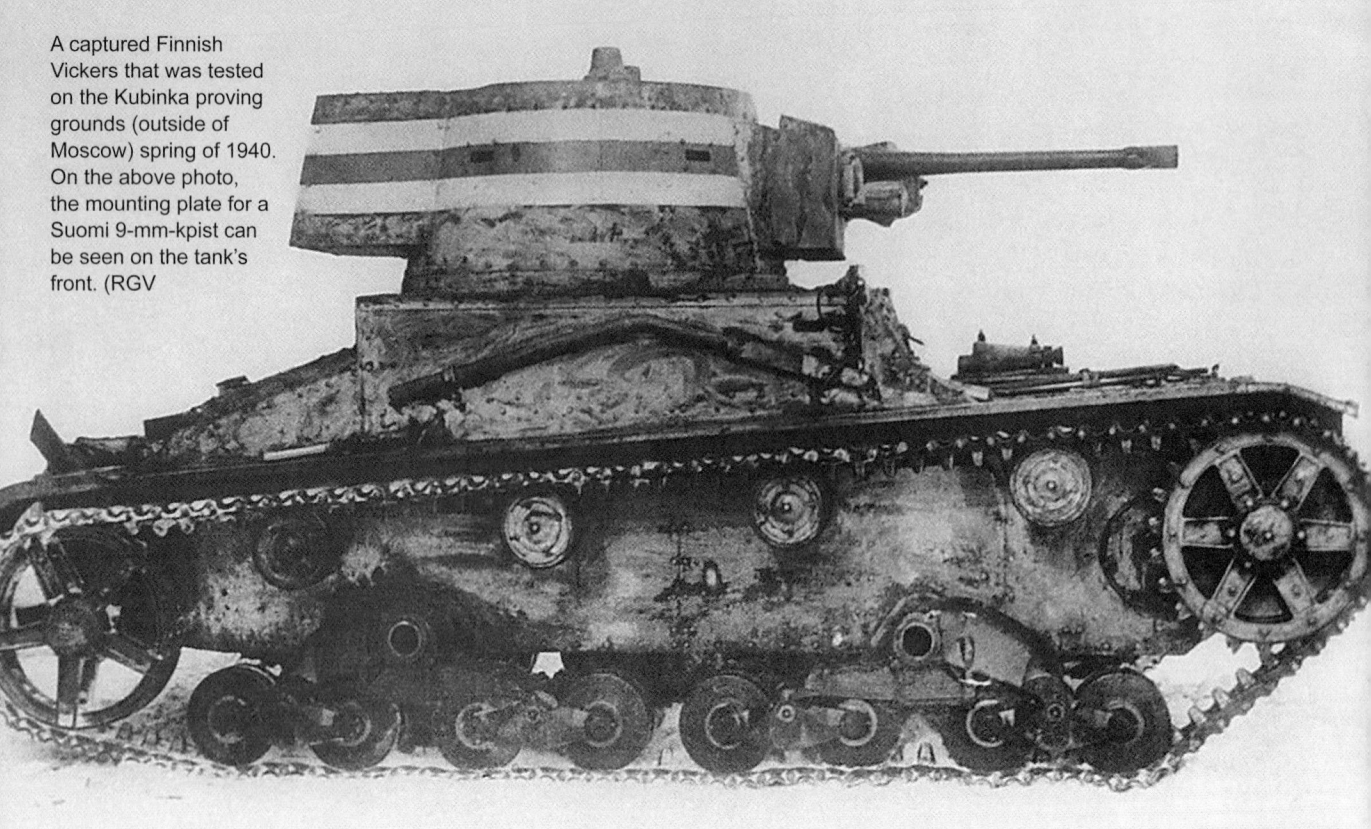

A captured Finnish Vickers that was tested on the Kubinka proving grounds (outside of Moscow) spring of 1940. On the above photo, the mounting plate for a Suomi 9-mm-kpist can be seen on the tank's front. (RGV

were well camouflaged and protected by a comprehensive combination of tank and infantry obstacles, usually this combination was carried out as follows – beginning with: three to four rows of barbed wire; 30-40 meters beyond that, several rows of timber or concrete obstacles; thereafter, another 20-50 more meters' distant, an anti-tank ditch or wall of earth; and lastly, yet another 20-50 meters' distant, a final two to four rows of barbed wire. A main firing emplacement (a bunker or earth construction) was located at a distance of 150 to 200 meters from the last obstacle. Nearby roads, approaches to the obstacle installations, and the obstacle installations themselves, were mined.

Anti-tank obstacles

The main, technically engineered anti-tank obstacles along "The Mannerheim Line" were barriers composed of stone, concrete, or metal; tank trenches; earth-walls; mines; and barriers built with timber.

With regard to the first mentioned, there were three types – stone, reinforced concrete and metal. Obstacles of hewn granite, measuring 60 x 200 cm, were dug into the earth 60-100 cm, or, as was mostly the case on the Karelian Isthmus, blocks of stone measuring up to a meter in diameter. They were demolished by the force of 45 mm tank grenades (3-4 grenades totally destroyed such an obstacle) or by being blown apart by engineer troops. Sometimes, if the tank driver was very skilful, tanks could be successfully driven over these stone or concrete obstacles. The reinforced concrete obstacles were shaped like a pyramid with a height of 80-100 cm and a base width of 60-80 cm. They were most often encountered along roads and, as a rule, they were not particularly durable – one of the tank crew would jump from the tank and easily destroy them with a crowbar.

Metal obstacles (usually portions of train rails rising to a height of 100 to 110 cm after having been dug into the ground) were only encountered in relatively small sectors within large obstacle zones containing granite or reinforced concrete obstacles. Tank obstacles of all types were laid out in a checkerboard pattern, separated from each other by 1-1.5 meters, usually in 3-4, and occasionally, in 5-6 rows.

Steep escarpments presented a vertical wall with a height of up to 2.5 meters, reinforced with heavy lumber or granite blocks. Tank trenches were 2-2,5 meters deep and 4-5 meters wide. The walls of the trenches were strengthened with timber or stone. These defence walls and trenches stretched over long distances (sometimes longer than a kilometer) abutted by lakes, seas, marshes or steep slopes,

A French 25 mm anti-tank gun shown in the "Crushing of the White Finns" exhibit in Leningrad, Mar. 1940. (ASKM)

Landsverk 182 armored car in Lappeenrannta, fall of 1939. The Finnish cavalry brigade emblem (crossed sabers) can be seen on the car's front armoured plate. (E. Muikku)

Bofors 37 mm anti-tank gun at the War Museum in Helsinki, (in Perejaslavtseva

Minefields were laid out along the shorelines of lakes and rivers (at places where tanks could make crossings), along the fringes of wooded areas, in forest clearings, as well as on roads and approaches into villages, towns and cities. In the main, three makes of mines were used: French, Swedish (with metal housings and 2-4 kilograms of explosive), and Finnish (with wood housings and up to 8 kilograms of explosive). Mines were set out in a checkerboard pattern, 1 meter distant from each other, along rows set 2-3 meters from one row to the next. Inside the security zone, the mines were laid out in double rows, whereas along the main defence line, the second (intermediate) line, and the rear line near Vyborg, the width of the minefields sometimes extended to as many as 15 rows. When tanks were disabled by French and/or Swedish mines, the damage was usually confined to wheels, tracks and axels, but the explosive force of Finnish mines sometimes blew holes in a tank's undercarriage and injury to its crew. During the course of military events that took place on the Karelian Isthmus, the Finns' exploitation of mines was an extraordinarily effective defence against tanks. And mined sectors were excellently camouflaged by the heavy-packed and plentiful snowfall.

The Finns even used barricades made of timber as anti-tank obstacles, blanketing roads, glades, forest fringes and the shorelines of lakes and rivers. These obstacles were constructed by sawing up tree-trunks into lengths of 1-1.5 meters, rolling them out onto the road and winding barbed wire in and around them – and, as a rule, these obstacles were mined and could cover an area 400-500 meters deep.

In certain places, tanks stumbled into camouflaged anti-tank traps in the form of pits, approximately 4.5 meters long, 2 meters deep and up to 3 meters wide – and here and there, tanks sank into very well hidden holes on the frozen surface of lakes and the Gulf of Finland.

All told, the Finnish Army's anti-tank weaponry at the beginning of the war consisted of only 112 anti-tank guns manufactured by the Swedish firm of Bofors. These 37 mm guns were capable of penetrating the amour plating of Soviet tanks of all types from a distance of 500 meters. During the course of the war, the army was provided an additional 123 Bofors guns, as well as a number of French 25mm anti-tank guns. The author is not informed of the exact number of the latter-mentioned but the total appears to have been quite small – on the March 13 1940, the Finns had 22 such weapons left after losses. The Finnish troops also made use of captured Soviet 45mm guns – of the 123 taken, they made use of 57 before the war's end.

In addition to anti-tank guns, the Finnish Army actively made use of anti-tank rifles sent as part of the total military aid provided to Finland from abroad. The author has no precise information concerning the total number, but on March 13, 1940, the Finnish army had 130 such anti-tank rifles, made up of three different types: the 13.97 mm English "Boys," the 20 mm Swiss "Soloturn" and the 7.92 mm German Mauser from the First World War.

Anti-tank guns were placed deep in the defence line and the anti-tank obstacles were directly covered by anti-tank rifle fire and specially detached units made up of two to four soldiers. Their weaponry included satchel charges, "Molotov Cocktails" and/or portable mines. The latter began as an ordinary anti-tank mine, but by placing it between two discs attached to ropes it could effectively be made portable enough to slip under the tracks of an underway tank.

In order to avoid premature detection, antitank gun emplacements began the practice of withholding fire until the tanks had passed the obstacles. In general, only a few rounds were fired from a given position, after which the antitank gun was moved to another location. By applying such battle tactics, the Finns won sufficient time to disable a large number of tanks without being discovered. Occasionally, field artillery cannons were used to fire on tanks but this happened very seldom.

Anti-Tank ditch on the Karelian Isthmus.

The most common way for the Finnish forces to attack Russian tanks, were to use a Molotovcocktail as we can see here.

T-28 from the 90th Tank Battalion, 20th Heavy Tank Brigade, about to attack, Karelian Isthmus, Feb. 1940. (RGAKFD)

2:2 Tank forces of the USSR and Finland

Organization of tank forces in the Red Army

At the beginning of the Soviet-Finnish War, the Red Army's armored vehicle forces already had a well developed organizational structure. In September 1939, it consisted of several tank corps, special tank brigades, armored-car brigades, the cavalry divisions' tank regiments, the rifle divisions' special tank battalions, special reconnaissance battalions, armored-train divisions, training regiments for tank forces, repair bases and training installations. A tank corps consisted of two tank brigades and a machine gun brigade, as well as a support unit. In all, there were four such corps in the Red Army, each one equipped with 570 tanks.

There were two types of tank brigades – light tank brigades, armed with T-26 or BT-type tanks – and heavy tank brigades, with T-28 and T-35 tanks. The light brigades were made up of either BT-type tanks (there were 16 such brigades, each having 278 tanks at its disposal), or T-26 tanks (there were 17 such brigades in all, each having 267 tanks at its disposal). The light tank brigades included in the total complement of a Soviet tank corps were made up of BT-type vehicles.

The heavy tank brigades (three with T-28 tanks and one with T-35 tanks) had 183 tanks at the disposal of each brigade.

Amored-car brigades (there were only three) were equipped with armored vehicles that had been designed for use in desert and flat-plain terrain of Mongolia.

In the cavalry divisions' 20 tanks regiments, each regiment had 64 BT-type tanks at its disposal.

The rifle divisions' tank battalions consisted of one company of T-26's (15 tanks) and one company of T-37/38's (22 tanks). In September 1939, there were at least 80 such battalions. A special reconnaissance battalion consisted of a tank company, an armoured-vehicle company, and a rifle company – in all, 15 tanks and 18 armored-vehicles. Official directives stipulated that a

T-26 tank crew getting a final briefing on their mission, Jan. 1940.

special reconnaissance battalion be included in the complement of every tank brigade and rifle division, but far from all of these units actually had armored vehicles.

An armored-train division was made up of one heavy and two light-armored trains, along with a platoon of armored-car inspectors. Altogether, there were 8 such divisions.

The 11 tank force training regiments had charge of educating the tank crews. At the officer level, tank personnel were educated at an academy and at seven special schools for tank forces.

In September 1939, the Red Army held a so-called "large education maneuver" and within its parameters, reservists were called up and new units were formed, along with the requisitioning of equipment from civilian businesses. .By means of these measures, two tank brigades were formed as training regiments for the tank forces – namely, the 34th and 40th Brigades made up of BT-type and T-26 tanks, respectively.

All told, the units called up at the beginning of the war against Finland were as follows: the 10th Tank Corps, the 20th Heavy Tank Brigade, and the 34th, 35th, 39th and 40th Light Tank Brigades, along with the 20 special tank battalions in the rifle divisions. During the course of the war, the 29th Light-Tank Brigade and a significant number of special tank battalions also arrived at the front. The fighting there led to corrections in the structure of tank units. For example, it became evident that the rifle divisions' tank battalions could not be used – under the conditions that prevailed on the Finnish battlefields, companies with the light T-37/38 tanks were simply not effective. It was therefore stipulated in a directive from the Supreme Military Commission for the RKKA (Workers and Farmers Red Army) in January of 1940 that every rifle division should be supplemented with a battalion of fifty-four T-26 tanks, of which 15 were to be equipped with chemical weapons – and further – that every rifle regiment should be provided a tank company of seventeen T-26 tanks. In all, 24 such companies were formed. At the same time, seven tank regiments were formed (each with 164 tanks, model T-26). These regiments were intended for the motorized rifle divisions (the 17th, 37th, 84th, 91st, 119th, 128th, 144th, 172nd and 173rd) and the light motorized divisions (often documented as motorized cavalry divisions, inasmuch as they were created based on the traditional cavalry divisions). At the front, these tank regiments could, however, be sent in with ordinary rifle divisions when necessary. Only two of these motorized cavalry divisions were actually formed – the 24th and the 25th. Each had at its disposal four motorized regiments (with cars and trucks), an artillery regiment and a tank regiment. The total number of trucks and tractors became significantly larger in these motorized cavalry divisions than in ordinary rifle divisions, and the total number of troops significantly less. As it happened, the motorized cavalry divisions proved to be disappointingly ineffective in Finland – making headway was a serious problem for many of their vehicles due to the poor condition of the roads,

At about this same time, five armored-car battalions were formed (each with 49 armored vehicles). The intent was that they could effectively press the enemy in retreat once a break had been established in the central, so-called "Mannerheim," defence line. But the terrain conditions prevented this plan from being successfully carried out, and consequently, the armored-vehicle divisions did not take part in the battles.

The Red Army's complement of tanks

The collection of Soviet tanks used during battle was very heterogeneous. For example, the 1st, 13th and 34th tank brigades were composed of BT tanks of all types – from machine gun equipped BT-2's to BT-7's of 1939 with conical turrets. An analogous picture was also apparent in T-26 tank brigades, which were equipped, both with vehicles having double-turrets and with vehicles having but one conical-shaped turret (In the future, for the sake of simplicity, we will refer to T-26's with two turrets as T-26, model 1931. In the case of T-26 tanks with one cylindrical turret, T-26, model 1933, and those with conically-shaped turrets having slanted armored-plating shielding the turret's underside, T-26, model 1939).

In the tank battalions attached to the rifle divisions, the equipment of the T-26's generally adhered to the older models from the years 1931-36. But certain units were made up of new T-26 tanks, model 1939, that arrived direct from the factory. Only the rifle divisions' tank battalions were armed with T-37 and T-38 type tanks – There were none in the tank brigades. To a large degree these tanks (especially the T-37) were severely worn.

With regard to armoredvehicles, all types were deployed on the Finnish front – everything from the new BA-10 to such "rarities" as the BA-27 and D-8. Armored-cars were a component of the tank brigades, of the special reconnaissance battalions, and of the newly formed armored-vehicle battalions. Even the armor-plated tow vehicles "Komsomolets" were actively employed in the Winter War. They were included in the equipment allocated to the rifle divisions and to the tank brigades' armoured-car

Bridgelaying tank, type ST-26. Such vehicles were used in the 35th Light Tank Brigade. (ASKM)

Bridgelaying tank, type SVT. Such vehicles were used in the 13th Light Tank Brigade. (ASKM)

Two shots from a weekly Soviet chronichle showing a SMK heavy tank driving to the forward assembly area near Summa in December 1939. The tank was equipped with extra tool kits and tarpaulin.

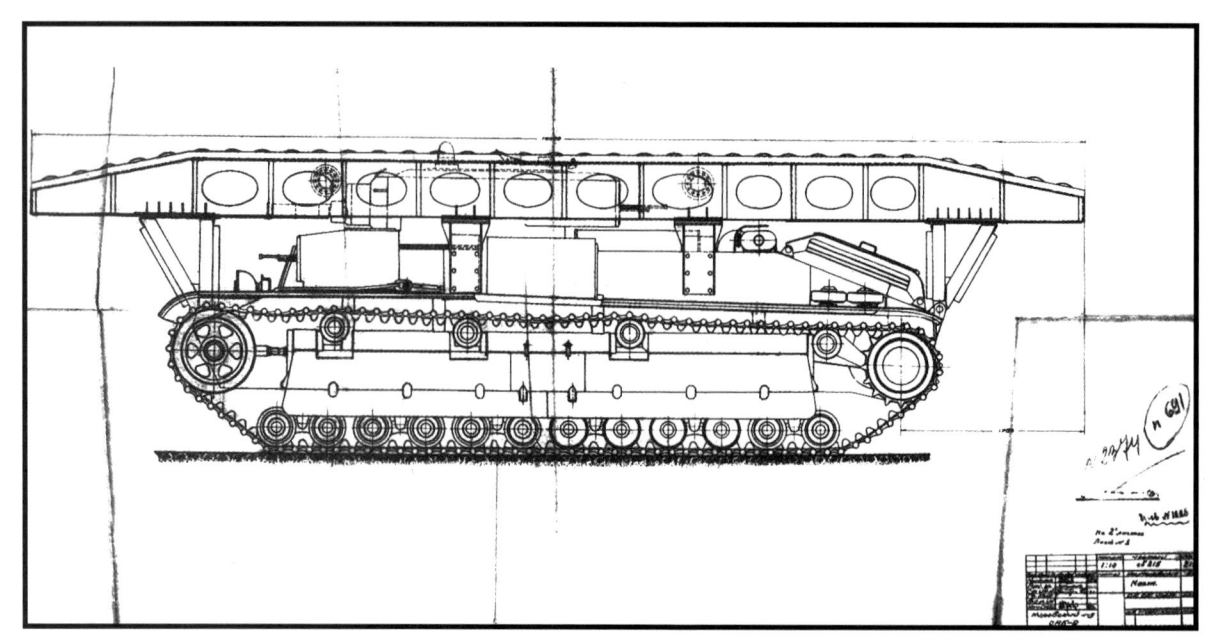

A projected metal bridge (to cross over anti-tank trenches) for a type T-28 tank (copy of the manufacturer's drawing). (CAFM)

divisions, and were used, among other things, for towing 45 mm anti-tank guns.

The small T-27 tanks were also put to good use. At the start of the war, infantry units assigned a large portion of them for use as tow-vehicles or ammunition transporters. However, the majority of T-27's wound up in sorry technical condition, and their ability to maneuver in the northern war zones was, for all practical purposes, zero. And yet, certain units succeeded in accomplishing their missions, and along the 14th Army's battle line they were also deployed to patrol the roadways.

All told, at the outbreak of hostilities, the tank units from the Leningrad Military District included: 108 T-28's, 956 BT's, 848 T-26's, 435 T-37/38's and 344 armored-vehicles. As the war progressed, the number of these combat vehicles constantly increased.

The Winter War is interesting in that an active use of certain combat vehicles continued throughout the conflict (among them, a number of small production-run series) that never came into widespread use thereafter. Therefore, it's quite meaningful and appropriate to examine them in somewhat greater detail.

Engineer tanks

Early on, even as tank personnel were being recruited in the USSR, its army command was already planning to equip the entire range of tanks with military engineering technology. In line with this decision, "The System for Engineer Tank Equipment" was approved in the beginning of 1932 – within the time-span of three years, the Red Army's arsenal included the introduction of tanks equipped for deploying bridges (so-called engineered tanks, according to the terminology then in use), tanks designed for minesweeping, plus a whole array of other technically engineer equipment (bulldozers, cranes, and so on).

In February 1932, a group of designers at the Military Engineering Academy, under the leadership of Engineer Gutman, began projects focused on creating a bridge-deploying tank. The first model of this vehicle, designated the ST-26 ("bridge-deploying T-26"), was tested during the summer of 1932. The basic platform for this prototype was a standard T-26 tank, modified by having a machine gun turret mounted at its center. An arched, 7 meter metal bridge was placed lengthwise over this and anchored in a special support mechanism. The purpose of this design was to enable T-27, T-26 and BT tanks to bridge anti-tank pits and water obstacles as wide as 6-6.5 meters, and overcome vertical walls and escarpments as high as 2 meters. The bridge could be set out over such obstacles with the help of a rope powered by a winch (itself powered by the tank's motor) within 25-40 seconds, during which the crew (two men) would remain in the tank.

That fall, a variant of the ST-26 with a foldable bridge was tested (It was deployed over the anti-tank obstacle with the help of a specially designed control frame), and

An S-60 tractor evacuating a tank that has gone over a mine. Note that the T-26, model 1933, is painted over in white while the Cht-26 lying in the ditch is not, Karelian Isthmus, Dec. 1939. (CAFM)

in March 1933, yet another ST-26 foldable-bridge variant was tested (this was an updated presentation of the first ST-26 model). In the summer of 1933, all three ST-26 models participated in maneuvers at the Totskij camp in Leningrad's Military District. Based on the results obtained, it was decided to start production of the foldable-type bridge, which appeared to be more reliable and less complicated than the other models.

According to a decision made by the Defence Commission of the USSR, industry was to deliver 100 ST-26 tanks to the army by the end of 1933. But production turned out to be very slow – During 1934, the army took delivery of 44 ST-26's and only 20 more the following year. By that time, combat forces had used the bridge-laying tanks, and they had proven to be unreliable: As bridges were being set out, the ropes often snapped off and the attached devices became bent. With this record in mind, the Red Army's (RKKA) Research Institute of Engineering Technology (NIIT), along with the manufacturer "Gipstalmost's" designers Vajon, Nemets, and Markov, developed the UST-26 model (*improved* bridge-deploying tank, T-26) with a so-called "lever-system." Using this system, the bridge was set in place with the help of two levers powered by hydraulic cylinders. Tests carried out in March 1936 revealed a series of advantages in favour of the UST-26 over the previously manufactured run of ST-26's – for example, the bridge could be folded back onto the tank without the crew having to leave the tank. But the new vehicle also had series of drawbacks.

Towards the end of 1936, the engineered-tank sec-

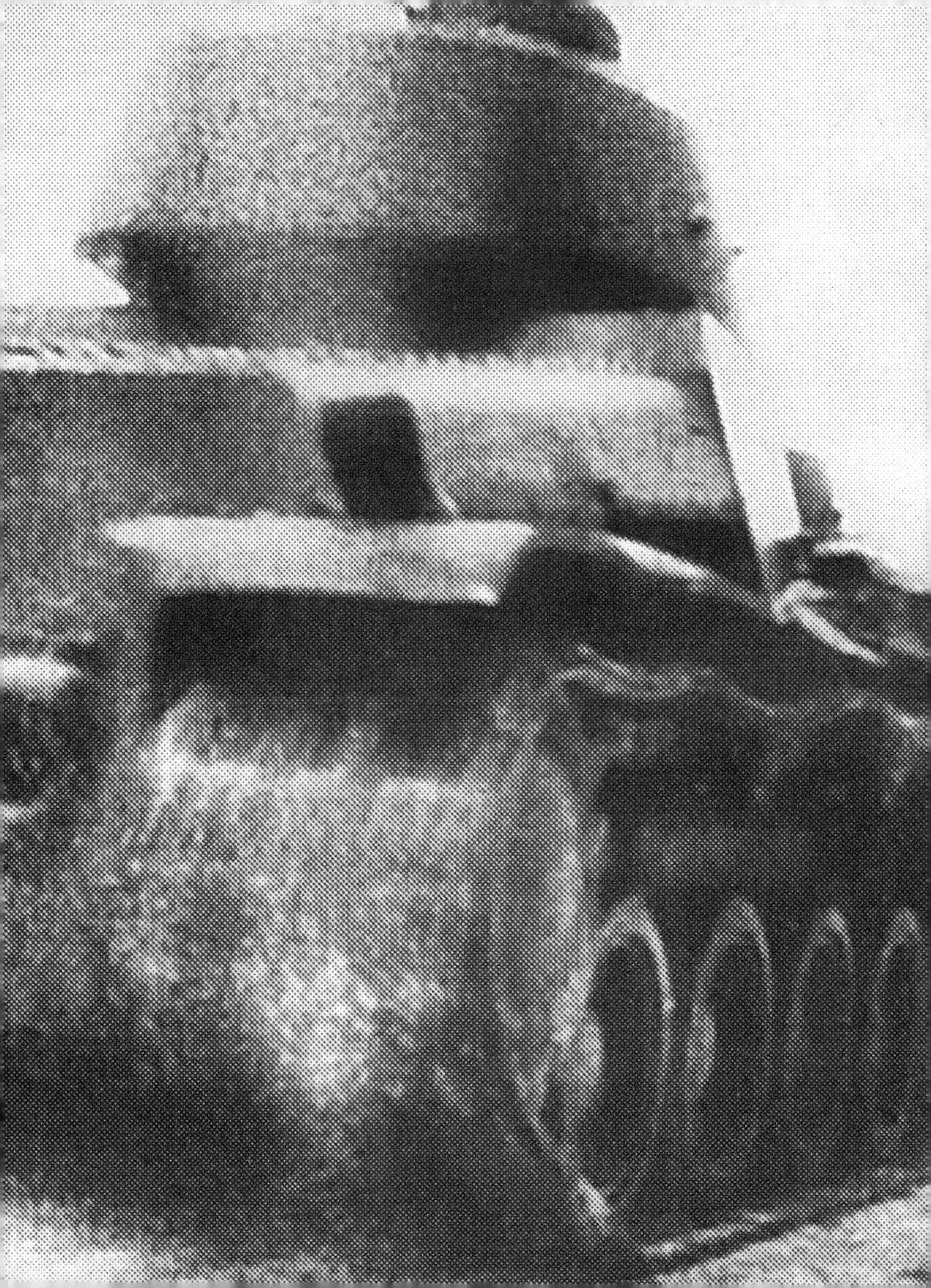

Two shots from a weekly Soviet chronichle showing a T-100 heavy tank driving to the forward assembly area near Summa in December 1939. Tank was equipped with extra tool its and tarpaulin.

tion at the NIIIT RKKA (the Red Army's Research Institute), which was formed at that time, together with "Gipstalstom" carried out a project aimed at designing an improved version of the bridge-deploying tank with the new lever system. The "Ordzjonikidze" machine manufacturing factory in Podolsk produced a prototype of this vehicle in July 1937, which underwent a period of testing on the proving grounds of NIIIT lasting until September. During this time, 85 bridge operations were carried out, testing the deployment and recovery of the bridge – with each operation as many as 70 tanks of both BT and T-26 models passed over the bridge. The following year, this ST-26 prototype was tested at the NII BT's (the BT-tank Research Institute) proving grounds in Kubinska and took part in tactical tank training exercises for the Leningrad Military District (LVO) demonstrating its ability to overcome man-made anti-tank obstacles. On the basis of this extensive testing, it was decided that a consignment of these tanks should be manufactured during 1939. But as it happened, by the end of that year, the Podolsk factory had only delivered one ST-26 with a lever-system.

It should be noted that layingdeploying tank projects were not solely confined to the T-26 platform. In 1934, for example, the leadership of the Red Army's Corps of Engineers began work on designing a 9 meter metal bridge for BT-type tanks, designated as the SBT (bridge deploying-BT). The following year, an SBT (built on the platform of a BT-2, without a turret) was tested – The test results led to the engineer-tank section of the NIIIT RKKA drawing up a new variant of the SBT in 1936 (again: based on the BT-2 platform) incorporating the mechanical lever. It was designed by the engineers at "Giptalmost" and manufactured at the Ordzjonikidze factory in Podolsk in May of 1937.

With this variant of the SBT, the turret of a T-37 was mounted on the BT-2 in place of its usual turret. And since the bridge equipment tied up much of the tank's upper surface, fire power was supplied by a machine gun firing through a port in the turret. Deployment and recovery of the bridge on the SBT was carried out without the crew having to leave the tank.

Over the course of testing at the manufacturer and on the proving grounds, which began in May 1937 and carried on through October, 81 bridge operations (deployment and recovery) were performed, with each

The first example of a model KV-2 tank before it's sent to the front, Leningrad, the Kirov Factory, Feb.1940. (RGVA) (RGVA)

bridge deployment having been crossed by 58 military vehicles. The testing demonstrated that the STB could effectively help standard BT and T-26 tanks to successfully get past various natural and man-made obstacles having a width of up to 9 meters. In 1938, plans were made to manufacture 5 SBT-tanks in order to test them with regular tank forces. But by the close of 1939, only one machine (built on a BT-5 platform) had been delivered. In 1936, the NATI began a bridge laying tank project based on the T-28 model (IT-28) with the intent of equipping the heavy-tank brigades with them. The work, however, was seriously delayed, and it wasn't until the summer of 1940 that the IT-28 was to make its first appearance.

During this same period, a range of other development projects were also being pursued: "mine-sweepers" for tanks, various wooden bridges and fills – made of trees and branches – to enable tanks to cross anti-tank trenches, special "mud-feet" and tracks for crossing swampy ground, devices for clearing away barbwire, curved bulldozers for cleaning off roads, and numerous other innovations. A great number of models were produced but none were taken into military use.

Thus, when the Soviet-Finnish War began, the Red Army's tank forces had no specially engineered technical equipment in its arsenal – bridge laying tanks were the sole exception: On November 30, 1939, there were 70 ST-26's (including experimental models) and three SBT's. But a total of only ten such tanks were on hand during the frontline fighting.

During the war, every tank brigade formed a squad, recruited mainly from the engineering forces, to clear away anti-tank obstacles. Certain tank units made use of bridge laying tanks – an SBT (with the 13th Light Tank Brigade) and ST-26 tanks, with bridge deployment controlled either by the lever or rope system (in the 35th Light Tank Brigade). The ST-26 tanks with the 35th Tank Brigade, for example, deployed two bridges during the storming of height 65.5, on February 18, 1940 – one spanned an anti-tank trench and the other an infantry trench – during the battle, these bridges were successfully crossed by the vehicles of one of the brigade's tank battalions..

Under battle conditions, the best results were achieved by bridge laying tanks that used the lever bridge laying system (an SBT or ST-26 from the Ordzjonikidze factory), while those that quite frequently employed the ST-26 model using the rope system proved to be unreliable, and consequently saw limited use.

Chemical tanks

On March 11, 1932, the Military Revolutionary Council of the USSR adopted a suggestion "concerning the handing over to mechanized brigades, chemical and other substances for combating heavily fortified infantry." In accord with this decision, the Command for Military Chemistry (VOChIMU) of the RKKA (Red Army) ordered that "a chemical T-26 test-model tank be developed and provided with equipment for dispersing smoke and flame-throwing, along with technology for dispersing poisonous substances." The task of designing

T-26 tank. model 1937, (with a conical turret atop a base with vertical edges) from the 39th Light Tank Brigade going on attack, Karelian Isthmus, Dec. 1939. (CAFM)

The place where units out of the 44th Rifle Division had been caught in of an encirclement – a T-37 from the 312th Special Tank Battalion with a 45 mm anti-tank gun in tow, 9th Army Zone, Feb. 1940. (Photo from the collection of E. Muikkus)

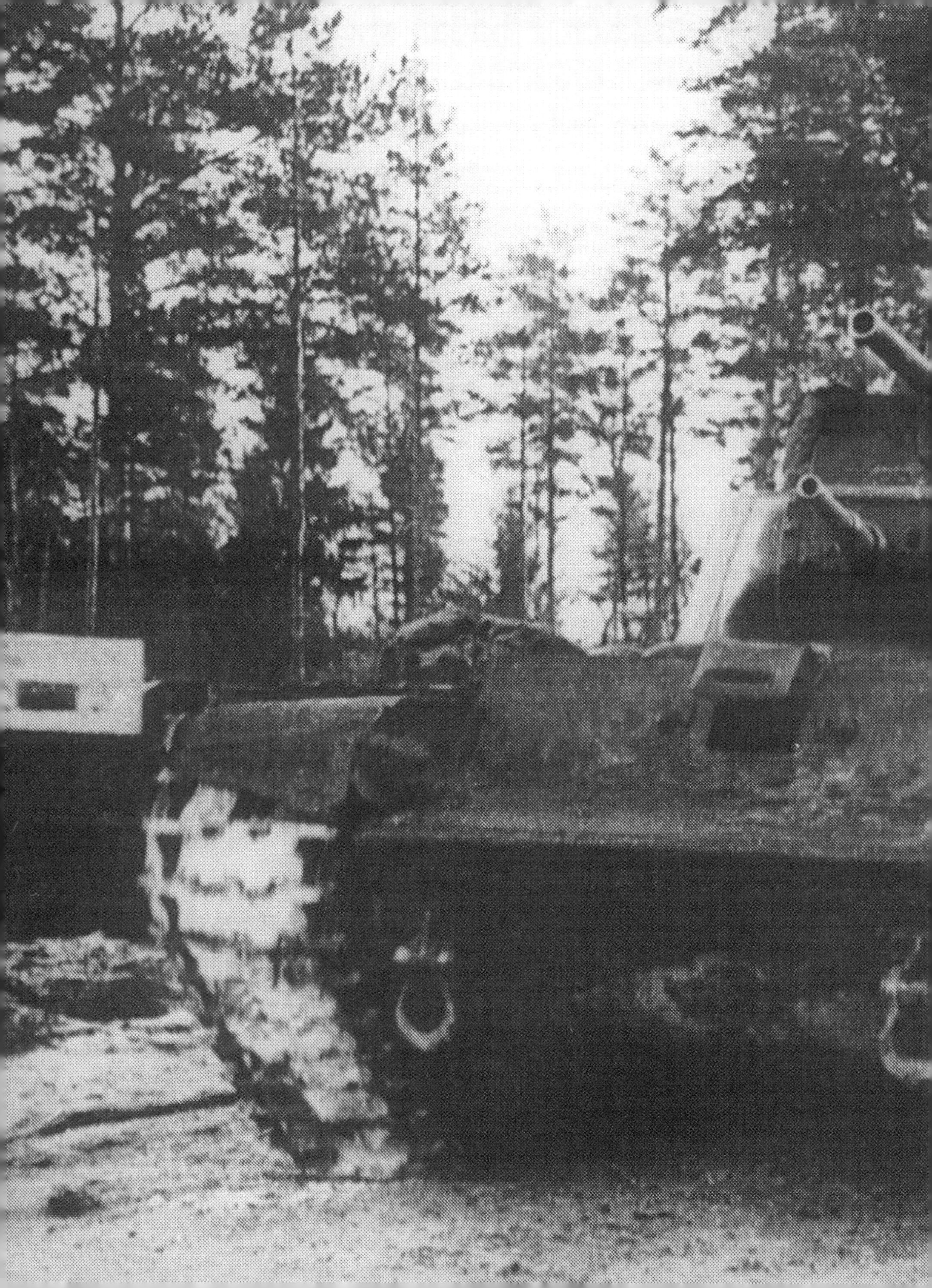

A T 100 tank attached to the 20th Heavy Tank Brigade, February 1940.

Tank unit meeting before a battle, Karelian Isthmus, Dec. 1939. The right fender of a T-26 tank is covered with a tarp. (ASKM)

the chemical equipment for the tanks was given to the design division of the "Compressor" factory.

The first model of the BChM-3 ("Chemical combat vehicle"), based on a T-26 platform, was tested on the Red Army's proving grounds for experimental chemical research beginning on June 1, 1932 extending through mid-July. Its starting platform was a standard T-26, model 1931, with the left turret removed. This modification left space inside the vehicle for a 400 liter storage tank suitable for holding chemical substances used for one of the following: flame-throwing, smoke dispersion, dispersion of poisonous gases, or the neutralizing of such gases – dependent on the tank's mission. This space also held three compressed-air tanks and a system of hoses and valves. A fire pump, with flame-throwing capability via a compressed air unit, and a DT machine gun, were separately mounted in the right turret. A sprayer mounted in the rear of the tank could be used to disperse poisonous gases, or a chemical mixture to neutralize such gases, or to spread smoke. The fire-stream from the flame thrower, which was mixture of diesel-oil and kerosene, had a range of 30-40 meters. The test results were good, and the following year the vehicle was adopted, under the designation ChT-26 ("Chemical tank"), as a bona fide armament (In documents from that time, two designations are encountered – BChM-3 and ChT-26. For the sake of simplicity, we'll be using the latter). In all, 615 ChT-26 tanks were manufactured over the years 1933-34.

During 1934, an improved model of the chemical-tank, the ChT-130, was taken into production. This tank was based on the platform of the T-26, model 1933. The turret of this model was moved to the right – and as with the ChT-26 – the special equipment was installed on the left. The design of the flame-thrower had been improved and the fire-stream now had a range of 50 meters. Up until 1939, 324 of these ChT-130 tanks were produced – thereafter, production was switched to the ChT-133, which was constructed on a T-26, model 1939, platform.

These chemical tanks were first placed into the armament of the combat support companies attached to the mechanized brigades (and later, the tank brigades). And beginning in 1935, they were also included in the armament of the special chemical tank battalions. These battalions, in turn, became additions to the respective complements of the chemical tank brigades. In 1939, there totalled three such brigades in the Red Army (In the Far East, in the Volga area, and in the Moscow Military District). Two of these brigades were also allotted a battalion of radio-controlled tanks, as these tanks were also armed with flame throwers. In the war with Finland – in addition to the chemical tanks of the combat-support companies attached to the tank brigades – five special chemical tank battalions – the 201st, 204th, 210th, 217th and 218th, from the 30th and 36th tank brigades – also took part in the fighting. In battle, the chemical tanks proved very effective in attacking Finnish fortifications. But they also proved to be more vulnerable than ordinary combat tanks, and suffered heavy losses. For example, included in the *Report concerning the Brigade's Operations, from the Command of the Motorized Tank Forces at the Finnish Front*, was the following: "In comparison to standard T-26's, the percentage of chemical tanks put out of commission is significantly higher. According to reports, battle losses in connection with standard tanks run 14.9 percent, as opposed to 34.3 percent for the chemical tank battalion. The explanation lies in the unavoidable eruption of fire when (hot) splinters wind up in the tanks holding the highly flammable fluid. If there is a large quantity of this fluid, fires in the chemical tanks continue to burn for 15-20 hours, reaching degrees of temperature so high that the motor's crankcase, the transmission, and even triple-plexiglass melt."

For this reason, some ChT-133's, put into use direct from the factory to replace losses, had reinforced armored-protection in the form of 30-40 mm armored plating. In addition, the flamethrower's short effective range didn't permit chemical tanks to reach targets more than 100 meters away. At the start of 1940, Factory no.174 manufactured two examples of the ChT-134. It was based on the standard T-26, model 1939, with the flame-thrower mounted in the upper front plate of the tank's bodywork. The heavy-duty canister, or tank, holding the highly flammable fluid was mounted on the rear plating in the box under the turret. Both vehicles were assigned to chemical tank battalions and saw action – one of them was hit. Meanwhile, the number of tanks at the front continued to increase, without pause. On or about November 30, 1939, the complement of chemical tanks in all five tank battalions, and in the support companies with the tank brigades, listed 208 ChT-26 and ChT-130 tanks. During the course of the war, 168 new tanks were delivered from the Vorosjilov factory (165 ChT-133's, two ChT-134's and one ChT-130), and from the Second Military District arrived an additional 70 ChT-26 and ChT-130's – in total, 446 vehicles. Of this number, 290 tanks saw action on the Karelian Isthmus, the rest were concentrated along the 8th Army and 15th Army's front lines. Of these 446 chemical tanks that took part in the war, 124 were disabled, 24 of them having been totally destroyed. Service to these tanks was provided by 302nd Repair and Service Battalion, which arrived on the Karelian Isthmus on January 18, 1940. By the end of the war, this unit had repaired 59 vehicles and towed 69.

From an overall perspective, the chemical tanks over the course of the "Winter War" were very valuable, despite their shortcomings.

Radio controlled tanks

In the USSR, they began to create "crewless" tanks controlled by radio ("tele-controlled" and/or "radio-controlled" tanks according to the terminology of the time), as early as the as the close of the 1920s, at the design department of the Central Laboratory for Telecontrol (TsLPS). On February 2, 1930, at a site not far from Leningrad, the first tests were carried out on the "Renault FT" tank, which was equipped with a special tele-mechanical device for remote control – "Reka- 1."

This radio-controlled tank (as with all those to follow) essentially worked as follows: A special device was installed in the tank to receive radio transmitted commands. This receiver device converted the radio commands into mechanical commands and – with the aid of compressed air servos – worked the levers and pedals that controlled the tank.

A T-28 belonging to the Northwest front. Feb 1940. (ASKM)

A radio-controlled tank from the 217th Special Flame-throwing Battalion destroyed by the enemy somewhere near height 65.5, Feb. 1940. The vehicle's bi-colored camouflage is clearly visible, likewise the two antennas atop the turret – a detail solely characteristic of T-26 tanks. (ASKM)

Over the following two years, intensive work was carried out aimed at creating functionally effective models of radio-controlled tanks and thus effective weapons for the Red Army. In addition to the Central Laboratory (TsLPS), the Institute for Experimental Research within Communications and Electronic-Mechanics (NIISEM), and the Special Technical Division (…?. Division) were also directed to work on creating radio-controlled tanks. The small T-27 tanks and the MS-1 and T-26 tanks were equipped with tele-mechanical devices. In the summer of 1932, with the objective of studying the possible uses of radio-controlled tanks in battle, a special subsection was formed in the Lenin Military District – "Section No. 4" – which, in January and October of 1933, carried out comprehensive training exercises with different types of radio-controlled devices developed at TsLPS, …?.. , and NIISEM. These training exercises revealed that the tele-mechanical devices had become significantly more reliable and that the tanks could carry out as many as 24 different commands.

At this time, a certain number of special tanks were built with the ability to direct the radio-controlled tanks. These consisted of ordinary tanks which, in addition to standard weaponry, were fitted with the equipment necessary to command the radio-controlled tanks (previously, all remote commands were sent from non-mobile instrument panels). The radio-controlled tank together with the "control-tank" made up a so-called "tele-mechanic group." In battle situations, the crew of the control-tank directed the radio-controlled tank over a precisely chosen route, and it soon became apparent that this method was significantly more effective than sending commands via a stationary instrument panel. It should also be mentioned that when the tele-mechanical device was shut down (and this didn't take long), the radio-controlled tank acted as an ordinary tank and could be manned by a crew.

In 1934, Scientific Research Institute (NII) No. 20, patterned after the NIISEM, was created in Moscow with the aim of carrying out further successful model-projects. It took charge of all work connected with radio-controlled tanks being carried out at TsLPS and --?-- . In 1935, the TOZ-IV tele-device for T-26 tanks was developed at NII No. 20: It tested well and immediately thereafter was put into service. By the fall of 1936, industry had produced 33 "tele-mechanical groups" (33 radio-controlled tanks and 33 control tanks). In accordance with a directive from the General Staff of the Red Army, the radio-controlled tanks were put into the heavy tank brigades of the Commander-in-Chief's Reserves. They were intended for use in searching for minefields and other tank obstacles and for exploring possible ways

Another KV heavy tank forefather, the T-100 heavy tank in 1939.

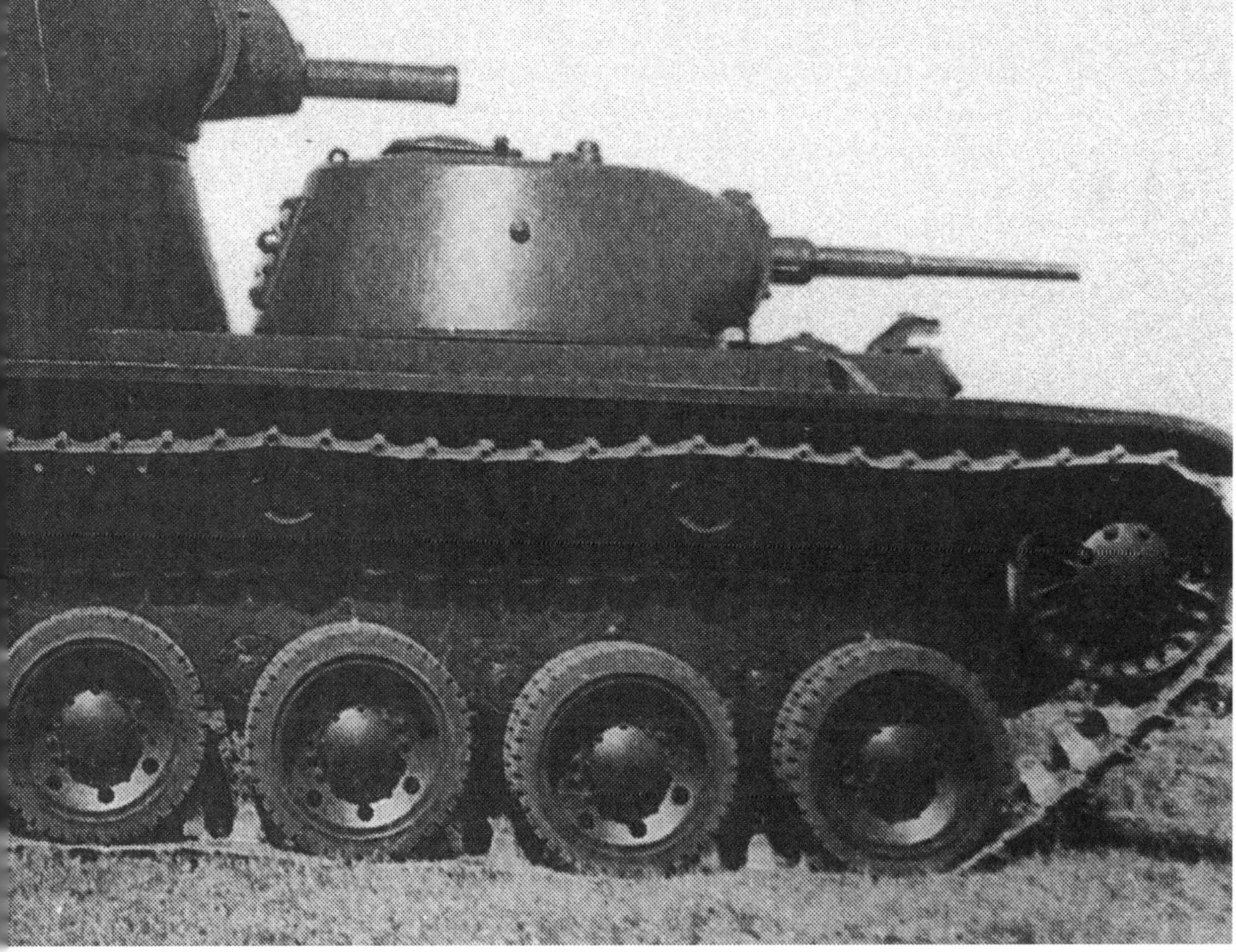

The KV heavy tank forefather,
the SMK heavy tank in 1939.

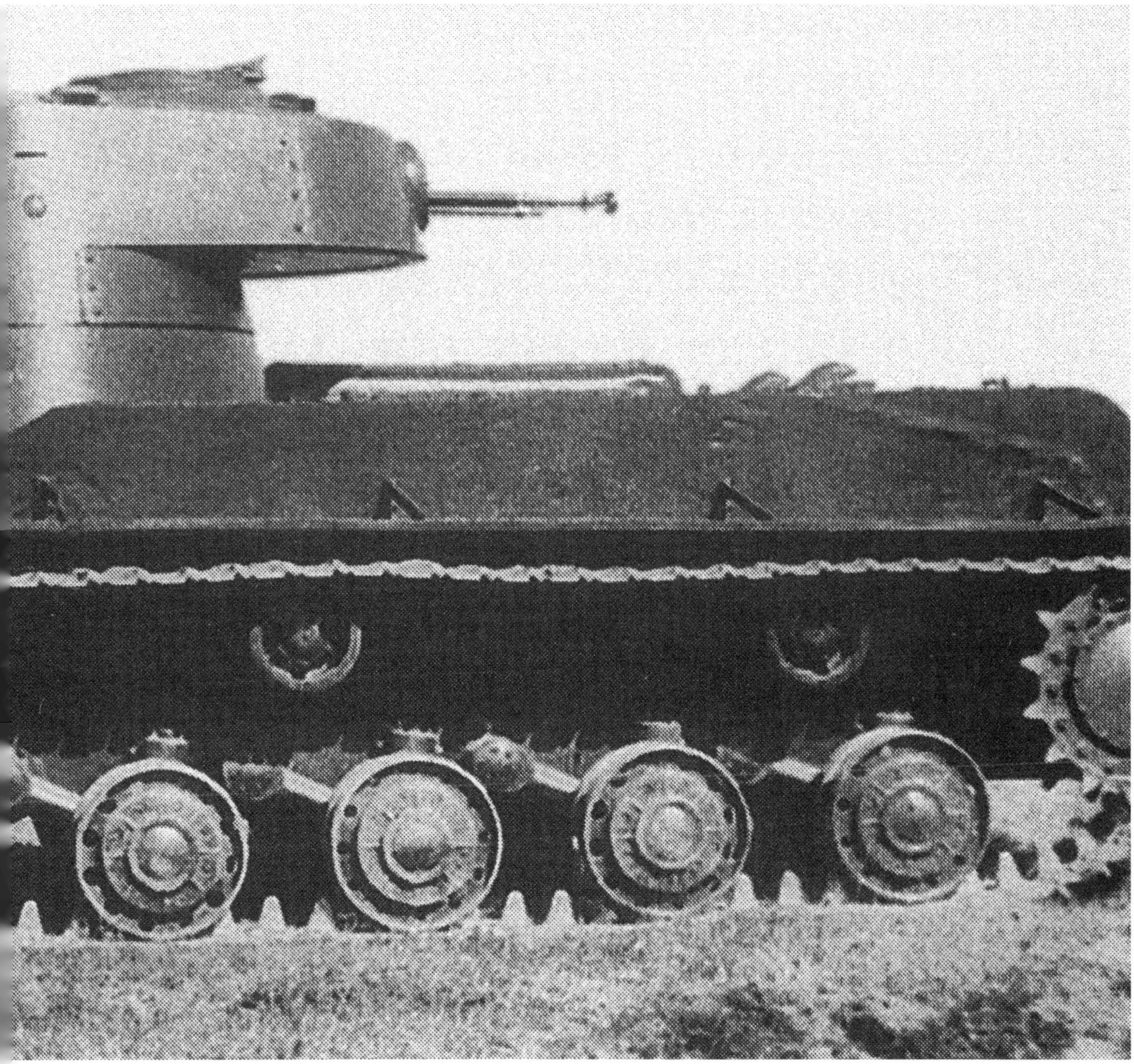

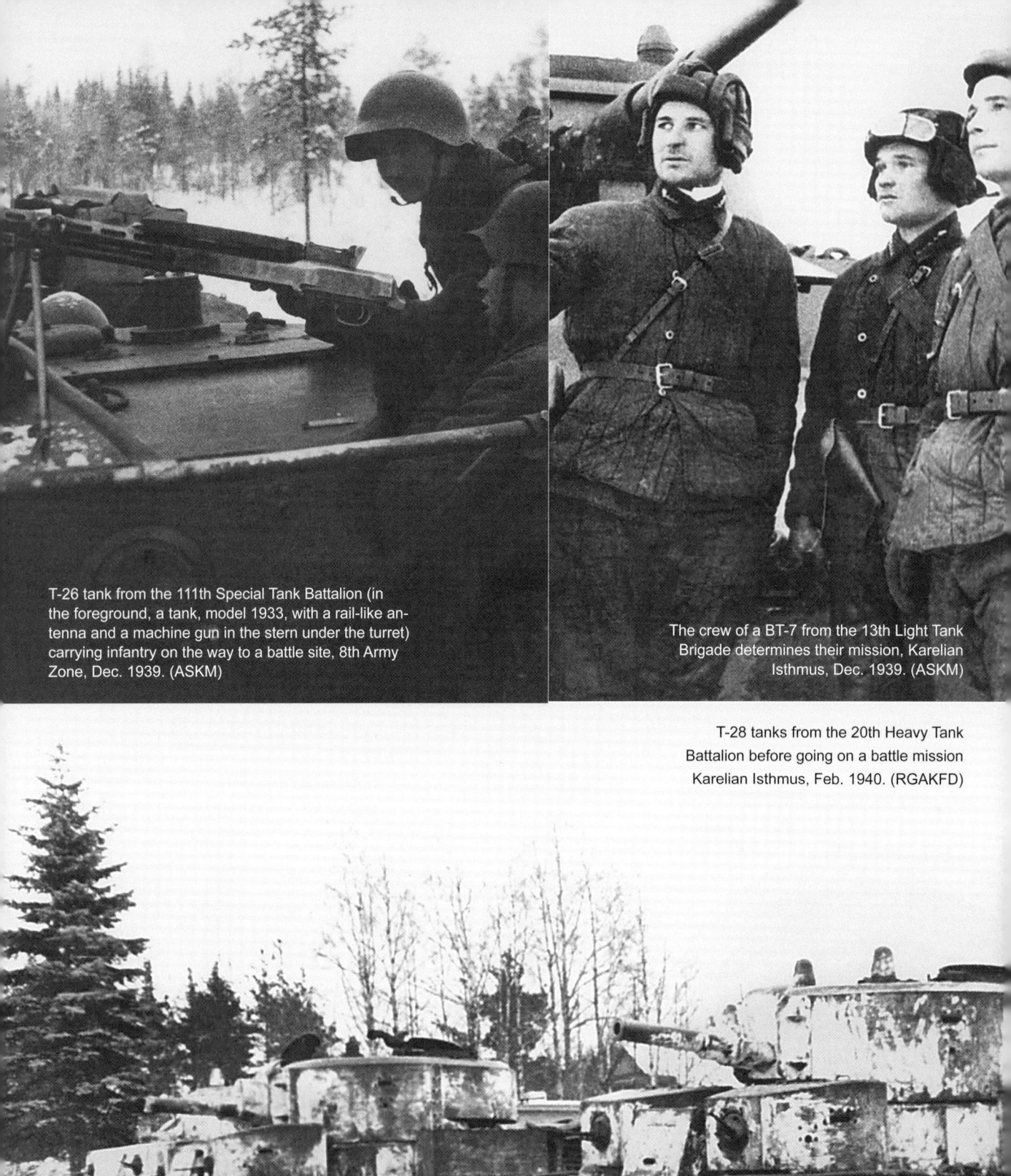

T-26 tank from the 111th Special Tank Battalion (in the foreground, a tank, model 1933, with a rail-like antenna and a machine gun in the stern under the turret) carrying infantry on the way to a battle site, 8th Army Zone, Dec. 1939. (ASKM)

The crew of a BT-7 from the 13th Light Tank Brigade determines their mission, Karelian Isthmus, Dec. 1939. (ASKM)

T-28 tanks from the 20th Heavy Tank Battalion before going on a battle mission Karelian Isthmus, Feb. 1940. (RGAKFD)

of getting past them, to destroy bunkers, to function as flame-throwers and to disperse smoke gases, as well as to function as rescue vehicles for the crews of disabled tanks.

In 1937, an improved model of the tele-mechanical device for T-26's, the TOZ-VI, was created under the leadership of Engineer Svirsjtjevski. During the following year, 28 tele-mechanical groups (56 tanks), equipped with these devices were manufactured at Factory No. 192. These vehicles were assigned as armament for two specially formed tank battalions – the 217th and the 152nd – which were, respectively, a part of the 30th and 36th tank brigades. The weaponry of radio-controlled tanks consisted of a flame-thrower and a DT machinegun. Their outer appearance differed from the ChT-130 by the presence of two antennas on the turret. In September 1939, the 152nd Battalion took part in the "liberation march" to the western Ukraine. Their tele-control feature, however, was never applied and the radio-controlled tanks operated only as standard tanks.

The 217th Special Tank Battalion (T-26's equipped with the TOZ-IV) and the 7th Special Company (T-26's equipped with the TOZ-IV) included in 20th Heavy Tank Brigade saw action during the war with Finland. But, due to the extremely hilly terrain and massive anti-tank obstacles, radio control of these tanks, for all practical purposes, never came into use. Attempts to employ these vehicles to blast Finnish bunkers were unsuccessful – Their weak armoured-plating was blown to bits by the enemy's anti-tank guns long before they neared their target. As a result, development work was immediately begun to create models that could carry out missions to blast obstacles and bunkers, successfully.

Therefore, in December 1939, the Military Electronic Technical Academy developed a radio-controlled "overland tracked-vehicle torpedo" – a little truck fitted with "mud-tracks" (length 175 cm, width 95 cm, height 74 cm, and a weight of 450 kg of which 150 kg were explosive material). Despite tests that revealed the torpedo's limited capacity to get by stubble, bushes and hollows, the Leningrad factories, "Krasnyi Oktjabar" and "Krasnaia Zaria", sent 100 of these torpedoes to the army's fighting forces between January and the beginning of February.1940. But they were never used in battle.

A column of T-28's from the 20th Heavy Tank Battalion on the move, Karelian Isthmus, Feb. 1940. (RGAKFD)

At the end of January 1940, Factory No. 174 (the Vorosjilov Factory) built an analogue torpedo. But test results were negative and the project was set aside.

In February of 1940, Factory No. 185 (the Kirov factory) presented the tele-mechanical group "Podryvnik" ("the Blaster") that was designed based on a project led by the military engineer, A. Kravtsov. The platform used was a T-26 equipped with a TOZ-V1, with turret and weapons removed. The vehicle was strengthened with reinforced 50 mm armoured plating and a reinforced wheel system. These tanks were fitted for use as transportation vehicles and for the deployment and explosion of special "tank-boxes" carrying explosive charges ranging from 300-700 kg. The vehicles themselves weighed 13-14 tons. On February 28, 1940, a "Podryvnik" group was sent to the Karelian Isthmus but never took part in battle. However, the sorties that were carried out by the 217th Battalion in the Summa District gave positive results – For example, an explosive charge of 300 kg completely destroyed a five-row anti-tank obstacle by creating a breach, eight meters wide through its lines. And a 700 kg charge placed near the front side of a bunker, totally blew it apart on explosion. At the same time, it became clear that under the conditions that prevailed on the Karelian Isthmus (i.e. heavily forested and very hilly terrain) it was impossible for a radio-controlled tank to follow an exact target direction – this required hands-on steering.

Kurtjevskus' motorized guns

In 1931, the self-taught inventor, Kurtievskij presented a project concerning a recoilless gun. The idea gained the support of M. Tuchatjevski and development work on this system came a long way. The concept was considered very appealing – a recoilless, large caliber gun could be mounted on a motorcycle, a car, or a motorboat. Under Kurtjevskij's leadership, different models, with calibers ranging from 37 to 305 mm, were created and tested. Some of these were manufactured as a series in rather large quantities though the guns had a number of weaknesses: Their creator, after all, hadn't even had an education in engineering. Subsequent to Kurtjevskij being victimized by repression in 1937, all work to do with his system stopped.

Included among the rather large series of recoilless weapons that were produced was the so-called "Kurtjevskij" motorized/self-propelled gun (SPK), a 76 mm gun mounted on GAZ-Tk type armored-cars. These cars constituted a woefully unsuccessful attempt to significantly raise the terrain capability of the GAZ-A personal automobile with a minimal of expense by mounting a third, so-called "extra" axle. Based on the notation (TK means Kurtjevskij's third axle), the inventor of this GAZ variant was the same Kurtjevskij of the recoilless gun.

Tanks out of the 377th Special Tank Battalion coming back from the front after battle, Karelian Isthmus, Mar, 1940. A column of T-26's, model 1931, (equipped with a light and a heavy machine gun) led by a Vickers captured from the Finns. Note that a total of three T-26's are painted white, the rest are green. (ASKM)

These vehicles were primarily intended for use in the reconnaissance battalions of the rifle divisions.

During the Soviet-Finnish War, only two such vehicles saw action and they were placed in the 14th Special Reconnaissance Battalion with the 44th Rifle Division. After this division wound up being surrounded and crushed, the two SPK's, along with their ammunition, became trophies of the Finns. And after these unusual guns had been test-fired, they were demonstrated, along with other captured trophies, to the foreign press. In the spring of 1941, one example of these guns was turned over to the Germans for inspection. The other became part of an exhibition at the War Museum in Helsinki, and remains so to this day.

All evidence points to the Soviet-Finnish War as being the only military conflict where use of Kurtjevskij's guns took place.

Finland's tank forces

The first models of armored-transportation– the armoured-train and armoured-car – turned up in Finland during the 1918 civil war. In 1919, Finland's Ministry of Defence decided to purchase a sizable number of "Renault" FT 17 tanks from France. By that summer, 34 of these tanks had already arrived in Helsinki (14 with guns, the remaining with machineguns). In the beginning of the 1930s, the military decided to test more modern tanks with the intent of replacing the aging "Renault." In line with this decision, three tanks were purchased from Great Britain: a "Vickers 6 ton" type V tank, a 1931 "Vickers-Garden-Loyd" light-tank and a small-tank, the "Vickers-Garden-Loyd" Mk VI. In 1936, an armoured-car, the "Landsverk 182" was purchased from Sweden. This vehicle was included in the weaponry of the cavalry brigade's tank squadron. In the summer of 1937, Finland ordered 32 "Vickers 6 ton" type tanks without weapons or optics. But for a number of reasons, the execution of this order dragged on and they didn't arrive in Finland until 1938-39. These tanks were then armed with machine guns and 37 mm "Puteaux" guns taken from the old "Renaults."

This equipment proved to be very defective. Consequently, 37 mm guns (psvk/36 – a variant of the Swedish Bofors gun, manufactured under license) were ordered from the government-owned artillery factory (VTT). But only ten tanks became equipped with this gun, and this didn't occur until the Winter War had already broken out. Aside from these main guns, the "Vickers" tanks were also armed with a 7.62 mm "Vickers" machinegun mounted in the turret to the right of the gun – and a 9 mm machinegun-pistol, the "Suomi." The latter was mounted on the front plate of the tank's body work to the left of the tank's driver and was fired through special aperture. On November 30, 1939, the complement of Finland's tank force included: 34 dated "Renaults," 33 "Vickers," an armoured-car "Landsverk," and a little and light tank, along with two armored trains.

Organizationally, tanks belonged in the Special Armored-Vehicle Battalion that was made up of five companies – the 1st and 2nd of "Renaults" and the 3rd and 4th of "Vickers" – and the 5th was a training company (with the little and light tank), along with repair facilities. In all, the battalion had approximately 700 men, the commander was Major S. Björkman.

Battles

Tank personnel and infantry review their mission, 8th Army Zone, Dec. 1939. (ASKM)

3:1 Battles on the Karelian isthmus

The general course of the war

The Karelian Isthmus was perceived by the antagonists on both sides as the most vital sector of the front. The main body of both forces were concentrated just here. The 7th Army, commanded by Lieutenant General B. Jakolev (from December 9, 1939 to the end of the war, K. Meretskov), commanded and dispersed the largest contingent of combat forces, consisting of: the 50th and 19th Rifle Corps, the 10th Tank Corps, the 123rd, 138th, 49th and 150th Rifle Divisions, along with the 20th, 35th, and 40th tank brigades. Their mission was to break through the Finnish defences, then advance to the Viborg-Kexholm rail line and join up with forces of the 8th Army that had launched an offensive along its section of the front in the direction of Petrozavosk, and thereafter launch an offensive towards Helsinki, all within a period of 12-15 days

Opposing the forces of the Red Army stood the Isthmus Army commanded by Lieutenant General H. Österman, which consisted of the II and III Army Corps along with the National Guard (in early December this unit was reorganized into the 1st Infantry Division). As the National Guard began to withdraw at the beginning of the war, they carried out battles that delayed the enemy, mined roads, built obstacles and made barricades of fallen trees. The civilian population withdrew from the front and a great many buildings were set afire to prevent them from being used by the Red Army,

Despite the Soviet's crushing, shear-force advantage, their offensive advanced very slowly, about 5-6 kilometers per day (less then half the planned distance). The few roads and inadequate organization of transportation led to congestion – standstills arose and many smaller units became disoriented. With nightfall the Red Amy forces ceased fighting and took to defensive tactics.

The largest gains were achieved on the Red Army's right flank, where the Finns were forced to retreat from the main defence line to the other side of the Taipalenjoki river and Lake Suvantojärvi. A decision was there-

A so-called "millions bunker" not far from Lake Summajärvi along the Mannerheim Line. Its measurements can be gleaned by comparing it with the soldier standing alongside, Karelian Isthmus, Feb. 1940. (CAFM)

fore made to break through the front at just that point. To carry out this mission an operation assault unit was assembled under the leadership of Corps Commander V. Grendal. It consisted of the 49th and 150th Rifle Divisions, a regiment out of the 142nd Rifle Division, as well as several artillery regiments. The assault unit's objective was to penetrate the Finn's flank and press on to position units behind their lines in the Kexholm district. But the assembled units couldn't break through the enemy's defence, and on December 8 the operation was called off.

On December 13, it was quite clear in which direction the Soviet forces were going to launch the main thrust of their offensive – along the main road and railway from Leningrad to Viborg. They planned to make a breakthrough with forces out of the 50th Rifle Brigade, after which they intended to strengthen this success by bringing in tanks from the 10th Tank Corps. Due to a regrouping of forces, this offensive was set back several days. On December 17, three rifle divisions, supported by the 20th Heavy Tank Brigade, attempted to breakthrough the Finn's defence in the Summa-Hottinen district and in the district of height 6.5 (in the direction of the town of Lähde). From the 17th to the 20th of December, intense and bloody fighting raged along this sector of the Finnish front. Tanks of the 20th Tank Brigade twice succeeded in breaking through the Finn's fortifications and advanced behind their frontline positions. But the Soviet infantry was cut off from the tanks and, without the infantry, securing the success that been achieved wasn't possible.

On December 21, the Soviet command clearly recognized that the offensive had died away without having achieved any goals. At the Finnish headquarters, this situation was viewed as a favourable time to go on the offensive and strike back at the enemy. To this end, the Isthmus Army was reinforced with the 6th Infantry Division made up of reserves. In the offensive that followed, launched on December 23, five of the seven divisions in place on the Isthmus took part. The command of the Soviet's 7th Army, however, took effective counter-measures and the Finnish offensive quickly came apart.

By the 27th of December, the battles on the Karelian Isthmus had come to a standstill. The Red Army command now realized they were not going to succeed in quickly crushing Finland. During the fighting, their

The crew of a type T-26 tank receiving fresh news, 35th Light Tank Brigade in the area of Perkjärvi, Dec. 15, 1939. (CAFM)

A T-26 tank, model 1933, crossing a bridge put up by the engineers, Karelian Isthmus, Dec. 1939. Atop the tank's turret sits a rod shaped antenna and along its side can be seen the fastenings for a rail-formed antenna. (RGAKFD)

A T-28 medium tank of the 20th Heavy Tank Brigade en route to the front in December 1939.

Finnish tankers driving a T-28 to the rear area in January 1940.

Hero of the Soviet Union N. Jestratov of the 90th Tank Battalion, Karelian Isthmus, March 1940.

Hero of the Soviet Union N. Jestratov of the 90th Tank Battalion, Karelian Isthmus, March 1940.

forces had suffered heavy losses and a host of failings had consequently become apparent in terms of leadership and provision of the troops, who had shown themselves to be unprepared for war under severe winter conditions. A decision was therefore made to terminate the offensive and serious preparations were undertaken for another attempt at breaking through the "Mannerheim Line." To achieve better functioning leadership of the troops, Grendal's assault unit was reformed on December 26 as the 13th Army. In order to co-ordinate the operations of the 7th and 14th armies, the Northwest Front was formed on January 7, 1940. The commander of the NW Front was Army General S. Timosjenko (I. Smorodov became his chief of staff, with A. Zjdanov and A. Melinikov making up the rest of his military staff advisory). Throughout January and the beginning of February 1940, intensive preparations were made at the Northwest Front to ensure a breakthrough of the "Mannerheim Line." During this period, the forces at the front were strengthened by the addition of 12 rifle divisions and a substantial number of other units (tank battalions, ski battalions, artillery regiments, and so on). All units made intensive preparations for storming the Finnish fortifications, and worked with questions concerning the co-ordination of infantry, engineer forces, and tank units. When the severe cold struck, specific locations for warming the troops were organized, and construction was started on building heated earth-shelters. In order to raise the calorie content in the soldiers' food at the front, beginning in January 1940, the standard norm for sugar consumption was raised along with the introduction of bacon fat and a ration of 1 dl of vodka per day. Meanwhile, Red Army units continuously engaged the enemy in small scale battles of only local significance in order to tire out the Finns, learn their defence system and destroy their fortification system.

The offensive along the Northwest Front began on February 11. The main thrust, as earlier, was directed along the main road and the Leningrad-Viborg railway. Battle engagements were hard fought. On the 13th of February, units from the 7th Army's 123rd Rifle Division, supported by tanks from the 20th Heavy Tank Brigade, broke through the Finn's central defence line in the area adjacent to height 65.5. A counter-attack attempted by units from the 5th Infantry Division proved fruitless. Looking to expand the offensive, K. Meretov gave the order to send an infantry-carrying, mobile tank unit into the breach (altogether, the 7th Army had formed three such units). By the evening of February 14, the breakthrough stretched 5 km wide and 6 km deep. The following day, Mannerheim gave his troops the order to retreat to an intermediate defensive line. On February 14, the central section of the "Mannerheim Line" in the 7th Army's zone had entirely given way.

T-26 on the Karelian Isthmus, Dec. 1939. (CAFM)

A light T-27 tank disabled by a mine, Terijoki, Dec, 5 1939. (ASKM)

The crew of a type T-26 tank (with a machine gun mounting from a P-40 anti-aircraft gun) watching for an enemy air attack in the area of Perkjävi, Dec. 15, 1939. (CAFM)

Evacuating a type T-26 tank that fell victim to a camoufl aged pit dug by the Finns, (th Army Zone, December 1939. (ASKM)

On February 22, forces from the 7th Army had penetrated almost up to the intermediate positions of the "Mannerhem Line" but weren't able to immediately break through them. The troops were exhausted after several days of fighting and there were supply problems as well. Timosjenko therefore gave orders halting the offensive, allowing the forces time to regroup. On February 27, the offensive was again taken up and the following day, The Finnish combat units began to withdraw to the rear defence line and the defence line protecting Viborg.

On the 29th of February, Timosjenko ordered the forces of the Northwest Front to " … completely break through the Finnish defences and crush the enemy troops defending the Karelian Isthmus." On March 3, the commander of the 7th Army, K. Meretskov, received an order to send units from 28th Rifle Corps (three rifle divisions, three tank regiments and one tank battalion) across the frozen Bay of Finland and cut off the road between Viborg and Helsinki. On March 4, units from the corps crossed the gulf and by March 8, the main road from Viborg to Helsinki had been cut off. The situation of the Finish forces on the Karelian Isthmus was very bleak.

On March 1, units of the 7th Army reached Vyborg. On March 11, they attacked the city. At that time, peace negotiations between the USSR and Finland were already underway. Mannerheim did not allow the troops to withdraw from the city and thereby risk weakening Finland's negotiation position. The Soviet command also continued its offensive and strove to make it clear to the Finns that the road to Helsinki, for all practical purposes, was wide open. On March 12, the Finnish leadership came to the conclusion that total defeat awaited their army. And in Moscow, in the night of March 12, they signed a peace treaty. The war negations officially came to an end at 12 noon, March 13, 1940.

The Soviet tank force's operations

The operational profile that was developed by the Red Army's tank forces on the Karelian Isthmus can, somewhat arbitrarily perhaps, be divided into three stages. The first stage – extending from November 30, 1939 to February 1, 1940 – encompasses occupation of the security zone and the way forward to the central defence line in the "Mannerheim Line"; during the second stage – from February 1-25, 1940 – after a period of intensive preparation, the breakthrough of the central defence line accomplished; during the third stage – from February

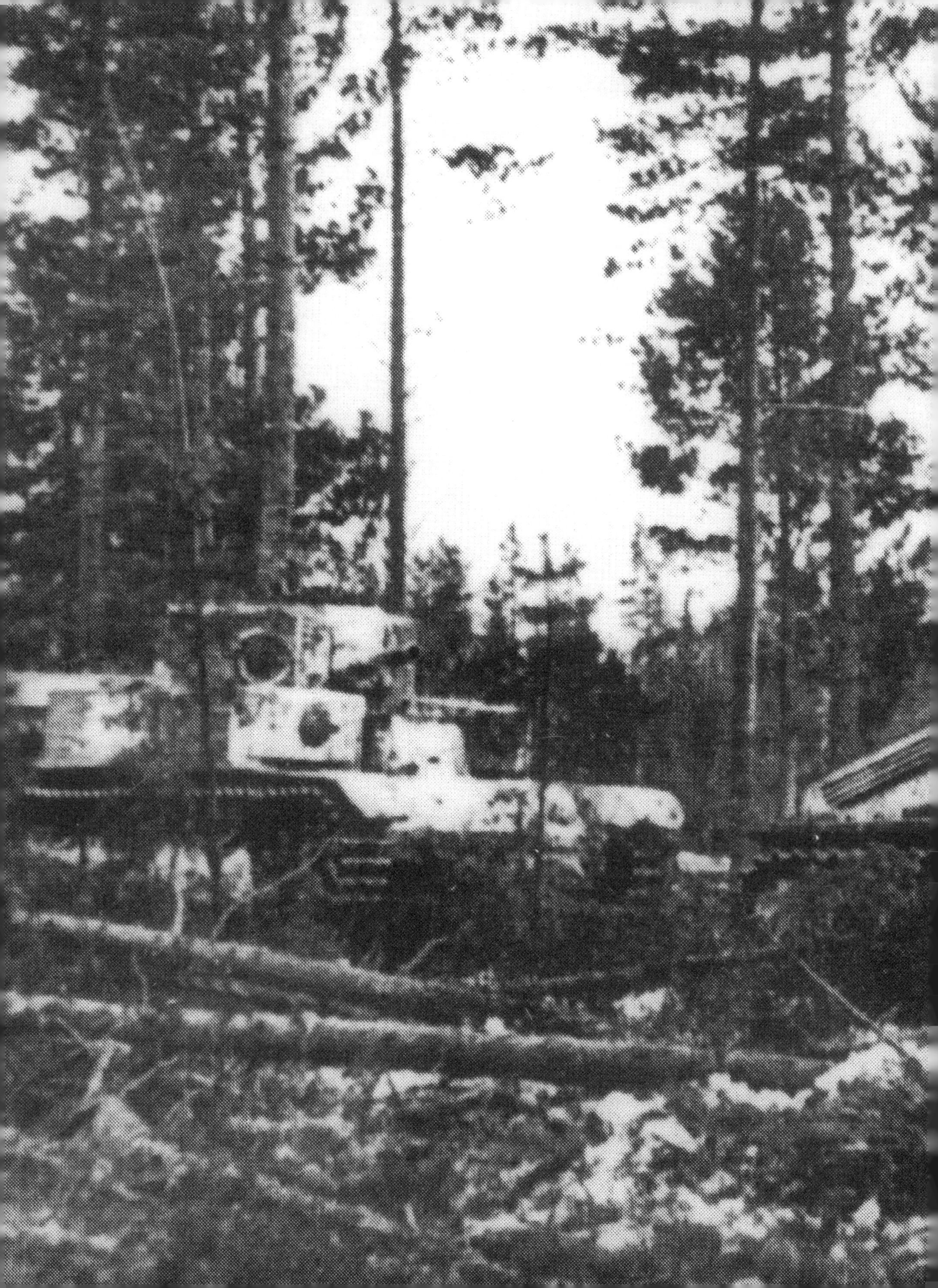

T-28 tanks of the 20th Heavy Tank Brigade en route to their combat position, Hottingen area, December 1939. Tanks in winter camouflage.

A mobile repair facility from one of the tank battalions at work, Karelian Isthmus, Jan. 1940. (CAFM)

T-26 on the Karelian Isthmus, Dec, 1939. (CAFM)

28, 1939 to March 13, 1940 – the breakthrough was expanded and Viborg assaulted.

Just prior to crossing the Finnish border, the total number of tank forces within the 7th Army's zone was fairly large. Nine rifle divisions were accompanied by a tank corps, four tank brigades and ten special tank battalions - in total, 1,569 tanks and 251 armored-vehicles. The 10th Tank Corps and the 20th Heavy Tank Battalion were used for independent missions and the remaining brigades were divided among the rifle divisions.

All tank brigades, with the exception of the 40th, which was formed from the 2nd Tank Brigade held in reserve, were professional and their tank crews well-instructed in flame –throwing and military tactics. The tank drivers were especially well-trained. The troops, commanding officers and political leaders, all knew each other extraordinarily well and this was a vital asset in combat situations. On the other hand, co-operation between the infantry and artillery was poorly developed and the reconnaissance units functioned badly.

The military vehicles were in overall satisfactory shape, but after having first marched back to the Soviet border from interior locations in Estonia and Latvia in October 1939, followed by a 500-800 kilometer march to the Karelian Isthmus, the equipment of a many brigades was badly worn.

As compared to the tank brigades, the rifle divisions' tank battalions went into the war relatively weaker and more unorganized. The soldiers and officers were not particularly well acquainted, and unresolved issues relating to co-operation had been addressed even less satisfactorily than in the brigades. The battalions contained vehicles of different types. In the main, these were older models and many of them were in need of repair. The majority of the infantry divisional and regimental commanders had no understanding of the nature of tanks and were unaware of their potential and possibilities. Therefore, it's hardly surprising that when the fighting first began, the infantry officers used their tanks to protect staff personnel and command locations, and for other special assignments – sometimes for bringing wood or guarding over bath installations – Tanks had, or so it was believed, "… the capacity to single-handedly lay waste to all kinds of fortifications and crush all kinds of enemies."

The first period of fighting was characterized by a "Polish" attitude among the troops. Many reckoned that things would go as they had with the "liberation march" to Poland in September 1939, meaning that the enemy's opposition would be minimal and that, "the relentless advance shouldn't encounter any significant opposition from the White-Finn's side." The vigorous defence put up by Finnish forces, however, forced the Red Army to

FAI armored car out of the 44th Special Intelligence Battalion, 90th Rifle Division going up a bank, Karelian Isthmus, Dec. 1939. (CAFM)

The crew of a type T-26 tank, model 1933, receiving presents sent by the laborers and office workers of Leningrad. From left to right – mechanic and driver S.Skatjkov, tank commander N. Sereda, political commander P. Bogrov (awarded the "Order of the Red Star" for battle on the Karelian Isthmus), turret marksman R:Mulasjev and mechanic/driver A. Lobanov, Karelian Isthmus, Dec. 1939. (CAFM) FM)

The first day of the war: The war's first losses – a medic helps a wounded soldier. In the background can be seen two T-26's, model 1939, with rod shaped antennas on the turret, Karealian Isthmus, Nov. 30, 1939. At that time the snow cover was light – The heavy snowfall began a few days later. (CAFM)

slow down the pace of its offensive as early as the first day. At this time, it became apparent that the infantry didn't, couldn't, wouldn't go on attack without tanks. During the entire advance to the central defence line, the infantry systematically trailed after the tanks. It was the tank crews themselves and more particularly the tank drivers who found a way over concrete anti-tank obstacles and earth-walls under the solitary protection of their own fire power. In the Lipola district, for example, the 35th Tank Brigade opened-fire against the special tank battalion with the 90th Rifle Division – the cause was the lack of co-ordination – as a result, three vehicles were blown apart and five soldiers wounded. For the same reason, during the first days of February 1940, tanks with the 20th Tank Brigade fired on infantry soldiers they were meant to co-operate with – casualties resulted. Questions concerning the lack of co-operation were not addressed until the breakthrough of the "Mannerheim Line" had already begun.

Over the first days of the offensive, the 7th Army attempted to use the 10th Tank Brigade to carry out missions on its own. According to plan, the tanks would advance to Kiviniemi, ford the Vuoksi River, then swing off towards the west and encircle the Finnish forces deployed on the Karelian Isthmus. The corps functioned like a brigade and reinforced the tanks with machine gun

Tank personnel receiving new years' presents from the factory workers of Leningrad. In the background – a T-26, model 1931, with a pile of branches on the rear deck for getting over anti-tank moats, the Northwest Front, Jan. 1940. (CAFM)

Type T-26 tanks, along with infantry, on an assault, Karelian Isthmus, Feb. 1940. The tanks are carefully painted completely white, even the roof of the turret. (ASKM)

battalions. Due to the massive lines of anti-tank obstacles that had to be overcome (presenting as many as ten rows of tank trenches and earth-walls, and 20 rows of stone and concrete anti-tank obstacles), the tanks didn't make it to Kiviniemi until December 5. By that time the Finnish forces had already set off explosives destroying all the bridges over the Vuoksi. The element of surprise had been lost and the brilliantly worked out offensive plan to forge the attacking tanks behind the Finnish front was impossible to carry out. The following day, the corps was transferred to the army's reserve.

On December 13, units of the Red Army arrived at the Finn's central defence line – the "Mannerheim Line." Attempts to immediately break through it failed – due to poorly conducted reconnaissance, the troops had no chance to grasp the character of its defences. In line with this ignorance, on December 16, the head of the 138th Rifle Division reported to the 50th Rifle Corps' command-staff that, "… there is no defensive zone facing them, the enemy had abandoned Hottinen and is fleeing." And thus, the corps' division commander, F. Gorlenko, gave the order, without having bothered to confirm this report, to halt the artillery bombardment, move off the roads and set out the 10th Tank Brigade to take up the chase. When the chief of the Red Army's armored-vehicle command, Lieutenant General D. Pavlov, was informed of this, he, personally, went to the battlefront and subsequently made it clear that the infantry of the 138th Rifle Division had retreated at night and that the Finns had then fired on and destroyed the artillery that had been left unprotected. With the aim of investigating the actual situation further, two tank companies were sent out and discovered the presence of fortified bunkers and anti-tank obstacles covered by a system of well thought out fields-of-fire. By dint of Herculean strains, the imminent attack by battalions from the 1st and 13th Tank Brigades was successfully halted and saved from very probable defeat.

On December 17, an assault made up of tanks and infantry was launched under the protection of artillery fire that saturated the area. But every attack met with the fire of Finnish machine guns and grenade launchers, at which point the Soviet infantry immediately deserted the tanks and fled in panic. And in those instances where the infantry had succeeded in securing one of the areas the tanks had taken, they drew back with the onset of nightfall. The infantry officers had so little confidence in their men that they left infantry missions to tank drivers, and ordered that such missions be carried out under threat of a firing-squad. According to reports from the 40th Tank Brigade's command, the commander of a regiment from the 24th Rifle Division ordered tanks to serve as night-watch posts – "…to protect the infantry located in an enemy anti-tank concrete-obstacle field and, if you leave them, I will give orders that you be subjected to grenade fire." And during the night of December 22, the 138th Rifle Division used tanks in their sector from the 35th Tank Brigade to defend the staff commands headquarters of the rifle regiments and the division against attacks from small enemy combat units, since the rifle forces had, in a haphazard fashion, abandoned their positions.

The attacks attempts in the Summa-Hotinnen district that continued until December 20 all fell short The main reason for this was undoubtedly the result of the infantry's inadequate preparation and its unwillingness to risk an advance. For example, this is what transpired on December 19 for two battalions out of the 20th Tank Brigade: After literally having "crept forward" under their own gun fire – clearing two zones of anti-tank obstacles, seizing a fortified central and advancing directly forward a further three kilometres – did, in fact, break through the main line of the Finnish defence. But when the tank

The crew of a type T-26 tank, model 1939, out of the 368th Special Tank Battalion. 62nd Rifle Division, before battle, Karelian Isthmus, Dec. 1939. Note that the roof of the T-26 turret, model 1933, standing alongside has been covered with a tarp to prevent snow from entering. (CAFM)

crews required that the infantry of the 138th press forward and occupy the bunkers, the Finns started firing grenades and the infantry fled in panic. At the time, the Finns were so demoralized that, for all practical purposes, hardly any machine gun fire was directed against the infantry. In the meantime, they'd marked that the tanks were carrying on alone, so they brought up their anti-tank guns and began firing them from the flanks and from positions behind the defence line. The two battalions continued to battle their way deep into the Finnish positions until nightfall threatened, at which time they drew back, after having lost 29 tanks.

All through this period, other tank brigades were being ordered to make senseless attacks by infantry commanders – resulting in heavy losses. In practical terms, nowhere did the infantry ever go on attack. On December 8, for example, an assault was about to be launched against Väisänen – and after the signal "To Attack!" was sounded, the 40th Tank Brigade began to roll forward while the infantry shouted "Hurrah!" from their positions, but they never followed after the tanks. The commander of the 112th Tank Battalion – humiliated by such infantry behaviour – asked the head of the political section of

BT-5 and BT-7 tanks abandoned at the location where the 34th light Tank Brigade operated, 8th Army Zone, south Lemetti, Feb.1040. (ASKM)

Type T-38 tank leading a transport column, Karelian Isthmus, Feb. 1940. (ASKM)

An armored cover being examined next to a Finnish concrete bunker, Karelian Isthmus, 1940. (CAFM)

The crew of a type T-26 tank nailing down its mission, Karelian Isthmus, Feb. 1940. (ASKM)

A T-26 radio-controlled tank, out of the 217th Special Tank Battalion, that has been destroyed by the enemy somewhere near "hill 65.5," Feb. 1940. The vehicle's bi-colored camouflage is easily seen, likewise the two antennas atop the turret – a detail solely characteristic of the T-26. (CAFM)

The commander of the 20th Heavy Tank Brigade, Brigade Commander Borzilov (farthest to the left) greets his tank personnel who have been awarded with '"orders" and medals, Feb. 1940. (CAFM)

A column of type BA-10 tanks on a road near the Karelian Isthmus front, tank unit unknown, February 1940. All the vehicles have been repainted in white and are without tactical markings.

how to battle alongside tanks. The infantry accustomed itself to using the tanks as mobile armored walls and in this way learned not to desert them when under fire. Many soldiers in the Red Army had come to recognize that enemy fire was overwhelmingly concentrated on the tanks and reasoned it was therefore safer to be a considerable distance from them when under attack. As it actually happened, in combat against the Finns the opposite applied, and Finnish fire-power an easy time cutting off the infantry from the tanks.

Seeking to scrap this preconceived view, a decision was made to place infantry soldiers in bunkers made of snow and have them site through the bunker's gun-ports, thereby forcing them to see the battleground from the enemy's eyes. "Now, see how the infantry creeps forward behind the tanks. Judge for yourselves who is easier to hit from the bunker – those who leave the tanks or those creep forward beside them."

The infantry's operations were severely hampered by the deep snow cover. But this problem was cleverly solved: When the tanks attacked over a snow field, every vehicle left two deep but narrow tracks behind it. The infantry successfully exploited these narrow paths by using them to creep forward behind the tanks, hidden from bullets. This method became SOP (standard operating procedure) throughout. In order to prevent foot-soldiers from being crushed, tank-drivers were ordered not to back up during an attack. In addition to participating in combat training, tank forces carried out battle missions of local significance with the aim of discovering and examining Finnish firing installations and anti-tank obstacles..

In total, the Red Army's tank forces lost 1,110 tanks on the Karelian Isthmus from November 30, 1939 to February 1, 1940 – of these, 540 were lost in battle and a further 570 due to technical breakdowns. A large portion of the losses occasioned by technical problems were caused by overloading, severe terrain conditions, neglect of routine maintenance and, irrefutably, the poor quality of vehicle repair in the field. Despite this, however, at the end of the first stage of combat, the number of combat ready tanks had been reduced by only approximately 35 percent, since many of them could be made combat-ready by repair installations. Tanks that had been incapacitated for technical causes were restored in full.

At the beginning of the second stage, the following were available at the Northwest Front: 1,331 T-26's, T-28's and BT's; 227 T-37/38's, along with 257 armored vehicles. The total tank force had increased through the rifle divisions' 20 tank battalions. The total number of brigades remained unchanged.

Flame-stream from a type ChT-130 tank from the 210th Special Chemical Tank Battalion, Karelian Isthmus, Feb. 1940. (ASKM)

Type T-26 tanks from the 35th Tank Brigade on attack, Feb. 1940. (RGAKFD)

During the period of preparation for the breakthrough of the central sector of the Mannerheim Line – which is to say, from February 1 to February 11 – the forces actively carried out reconnaissance by means of initiating a series of special large scale battle operations. Particularly heavy fighting developed in the fortified district of Hottinen, where battalions out of the 20th and 35th tank brigades advanced while giving support to units from the 100th Rifle Division, demolishing a significant number of bunkers and mapping out the entire Finnish fortification system. Despite heavy losses (the 29th Tank Brigade alone lost 59 tanks there), the main consequence of these attacks in the Hottinen district was that they forced the Finnish command to send over troops from other sectors, thereby helping to promote the eventual breakthrough of the central defence line in the area of height 65.5.

For the most part, during this period Soviet tanks were deployed in close co-operation with the infantry, artillery and engineer troops in battles that ranged over the terrain immediately before them and into the enemy's tactical deep defence. One of the most vital goals of such combat missions was met by incorporating tanks as an integral part of the blockade units (storm squads) assigned to taking and destroying fortified enemy bunkers. As a rule, such units consisted of five tanks (three tanks with guns and two with flamethrowers), an engineer platoon, up to a company of infantrymen, two-three machine guns and one or two artillery canons. Most often, the missions took place at night or during a snowstorm. Explosive material – it took from 1,000 to 3,000 kg to blow up a bunker – was transported to the object target by tanks on a surface of reinforced armoured (type Sokolov) leather. Tanks equipped with guns were responsible providing the fire power needed to allow flame-throwing tanks to come within range of targeted bunkers and spurt streams of fire over their machine gun apertures and doors, ideally, setting them on fire. Throughout this second stage, engineer troops set the explosives while the regular infantry protected them from being cut down by the Finns.

The first assault attempts made by these storm units were not successful. The problem was they were only going after individual bunkers, allowing the remaining fortified emplacements in the combat area to fire at will and knock out the tanks. Subsequent assaults – where 3-4 near lying bunkers were simultaneously attacked – were

A type ChT-26 tank out of the 210th Special Chemical Tank Battalion in battle, the Northwest Front, Feb. 1940. (ASKM)

Crews of T-28 tanks receive New year gifts sent to them from the workers in Leningrad, December 1940.

Politruk Bragin holds political information meeting with tankers of the 90th Battalion in February 1940.

A T-28 tank of the 91st Battalion 20th Brigade, destroyed on Hill 65.5 in December 1939.

T-28 tanks of the 20th Heavy Tank Brigade on route to their combat position, January 1940 Note that the tank is armed with a 7,62 cm L-10 gun.

considerably more successful. Especially good results were achieved by the 39th and 20th Tank Brigades.

Thanks to reconnaissance that was carried out through the co-ordinated efforts of tank units and other combat forces, on February 11, 1940, two battalions out of the 20th and 35th Tank Brigades, accompanied by infantry forces from the 123rd Rifle Division, broke through the Finnish central defence line in the district of height 65.5. Immediately thereafter, all the tanks of the 20th Tank Brigade were sent into the breakthrough sector and with their help the breach was widened and deepened. By the evening of February 16, the entire central sector of the Finn's most vital defence line, "the Mannerheim Line," had been broken.

At this time the command of Northwest Front decided form temporary mobile units utilizing tanks to pursue the retreating enemy forces. By the 14th of February, three of such groups had been formed:

Brigade Commander Verjinin's unit – 6th Tank Battalion from the 13th Tank Brigade, and a machine gun battalion – were assigned the mission of overtaking the Leipäsuo train station. On February 14, the unit came up against anti-tank obstacles and heavy resistance from the Finns. Under attack, they continued to their advance towards Leipäsuo but couldn't achieve their objective until February 17. At that time, only seven battle ready vehicles of 46 remained.

Colonel Baranov's unit – 13th Tank Brigade (less a battalion) and the 15th Machine Gun Brigade (less a battalion) – were assigned the mission of overtaking the Kämärä train station to further ensure the 123rd Rifle Division's success. After having broken through Finnish opposition at Lähde, the attack force continued its offensive towards Kämärä, which it took after battle on February 16. The unit's attempts to advance further were halted by Finnish gun fire and counter attacks.

Brigade Commander Borzilov's unit – the 1st and 20th Tank Brigades and two rifle battalions – on February 16, this unit undertook the mission of crushing Finnish forces in the Vipura district and of cutting off their retreat from the south-eastern section of the isthmus. The mobile assault unit reached Käräma on February 17 and on the 18th it began a two pronged offensive: The 1st Tank Brigade advanced towards Pien-Pero and the 20th Tank Brigade towards Honkaniemi. After having encountered hard resistance from the Finns, both brigades continued to battle, suffering heavy losses until February 20. Thereafter, the 1st Tank Brigade was transferred to the reserves for equipment repair, while the 20th Brigade, together with the 123rd Rifle Division, continued its offensive in the Honkaniemi district.

In all these cases, the mobile units' lack of success was in great part due to the terrain conditions and the character of the enemy's fortified installations, which not only hindered the tank brigades but also the tank battalions from carrying out their combat assignments.

Over February 23-25, units out of the Red Army, after having forced their way through isolated enemy installations, reached the second defence line in the "Mannerheim Line." These forces, however, couldn't carry out an immediate breakthrough. Instead, the offensive was brought to a halt in order to regroup and call in reserves. Total losses at the Northwest Front during the period February 1-25, 1940 mounted to 1,158 tanks, of which 746 were lost in battle and 411 due to technical causes.

After threes days' halt, on February 28, 1940, the Soviet forces commenced storming the second defence line. The breakthrough came on March 2.

In addition to providing infantry support, tanks were used in relatively small mobile units - a tank battalion or a tank company, together with an infantry commando unit which was transported in trucks or on tanks. The primary mission of these units was to expand the breach, cut off avenues of retreat, and encircle and crush small enemy units.

In addition, up until February 28, preparations were carried out in the section where the 23rd Rifle Corps, a combined-force combat unit under the leadership of the 39th Tank Brigade's commander, Colonel D. Leljusjenko, was to launch its offensive. The unit's objective was to occupy the Heinjoki railway station.

Leljussjenko took all measures necessary to prepare the unit for its contribution in the breakthrough sector, and this included personally reconnoitering the area from the air. A plan was worked out to co-ordinate his unit's offensive with the artillery, sectors of fire for the attack were determined, as well as a system for readying his troops for open and cease fire commands. As a result, his unit crushed the oppositions forces at Heikurila, and March 1, 1940, the Heinjoki railway station was occupied, which materially contributed to the successful advance of the 23rd Rifle Corps..

In March 1940 the tank brigades continued to follow up on the success of working in close co-operation with divisions from the rifle corps on joint operations.

On March 10, the Red Army forces, to all intents and purposes, had completely broken through the "Mannerheim Line" and units out of the 34th Rifle Corps began engaging in battles aimed at taking Viborg. The 29th Tank Brigade actively participated in the coming full assault of the city over the days March 12-13. In the beginning of March, the 29th Tank Brigade was formed,

A typical propaganda photo of that time – delivering fresh copies of the magazine "To the Homeland's Honor!" to the communications battalion, !st Light Tank Brigade, February 1940. In the background are two BA-10 tanks.

consisting of three rifle divisions, three tank regiments, and a tank battalion (261 tanks in all). Its mission was to cross the iced-over Gulf of Finland and wreck havoc on enemy positions defending Viborg by attacking them from the rear.

The contributions of the 28th and 62nd Tank Regiments to this plan were especially successful. On March 5, despite a snowstorm and bitter -30 degree cold, they crossed the iced-over Gulf of Finland and established, after having rid the islands of Finnish forces, a beachhead on the mainland.

At the end of the war – March 13, 1940 – the tank crews helped the infantry to expand this base point by cutting off the main Viborg-Helsinki roadway.

Altogether, from November 30, 1939 until March 13, 1940, units out of the 7th and 13th Armies on the Karelian Isthmus lost 3,178 tanks – of these, 1,903 were lost in battle, and 1,275 due to technical causes. If these figures are compared to the reported average total of 1,500 tanks on the Karelian Isthmus over the course of the war, then it appears that, on average, every tank was put out action twice, repaired and set back into combat (see table 1).

A few words concerning the living conditions of the tank crews on the Karelian Isthmus: Under the severe winter cold and with no access to indoor lodging, finding a likely place to survive the night, even an earth shelter or a vehicle specially warmed-up for common use, was not always possible – far from it. The tanks were too compact, and if the motor was shut down, the tanks became too cold and if they were allowed to idle they became too hot. But the tank crews improvised a solution: They hung the tarp normally used to shield the tank from severe weather from the tank's turret so that it formed a cover, or "tent," over the engine section's armor-plating. To warm-up the "tent" the warm air streaming from the engine's vents was directed, with the help of a special screen, under the tarp. Sometimes, these "tents" were provided with lighting powered by the tanks' storage batteries. With the help of these same tarps baths could be set up – The tent was raised directly on the snow or ice, a passable ground surface provided and held warm by hay, fir branches and wooden planks and, instead of an oven, hot water was held in gas cans and poured into ammunition boxes made of zinc

Material and technical support

In order to improve the supply of fuel, grease and spare-parts to the tank forces, as well as the towing and repair of disabled tanks, a Northwest Front Command for Technical Military Support was duly created, on January 10, 1940. Despite the incredibly difficult working conditions, and the need for a greater number of tanks (of the stipulated 2,932 tanks, only 766 were in place) this command was able to continually re-supply fuel to the tank units during the entire time the war was in progress. It should also be noted that throughout the entire war, the lack of spare-parts for the tanks was very telling, especially for the T-26. Despite this, the tank units, making use of their own resources, were able to carry out 9, 200 routine services and 745 intermediate level repairs of combat vehicles under wartime conditions. In January 1940, the repair and service battalions of the tank brigades were strengthened with the addition of special work-brigades from the manufacturers in Leningrad ("Kirovverken" and Factory no. 174 at Vorosjilovverken). These brigades provided great assistance with needed tank repairs.

Where comprehensive repairs were needed, the Leningrad manufacturers were called upon. These included: Kirovverken, Factory no. 174 and the Kirov factory for lift and transport equipment (in all, 857 combat vehicles were sent to the manufacturers). The performance of Kirovverken was especially noteworthy – The rest managed to raise their repair capacity but not to a level that could satisfy the demands at the front. In addition, in January 1940, a series of closely spaced electrical breakdowns at the factories caused many repairs to be set aside.

In December 1939, the total number of tank-repair facilities was increased by establishing repair centers no.

TABEL 1: LOSSES AND RESTORATION BY SUPPORT UNITS FOR THE 7TH ARMY'S TANK FORCES FROM NOVEMBER 30, 1939 TO MARCH 13, 1940

Type of tank	T-28	BT	T-26	T-37	T-38
Lost after the outbreak of war	482	956	930	97	78
Total number repaired during the war	386	582	463	5	62

TABEL 2. LOSSES OF THE RED ARMY'S TANK FORCES ON THE KARELIAN ISTHMUS FROM NOVEMBER 30 1939 UNTIL MARCH 13 1940.

Period	Army	Losses						Of said losses –the no. restored
		Due to:. art.fire	mines	fire	Under water	Vanished w/o trace	Tech.. causes	
Fr. 30.11.39 till 01.02.40	7A	199	90	92	13	1	375	62
	13A	76	16	62	-	1	195	56
Fr. 01.02.40 till 25.02.40	7A	264	137	84	43	9	259	96
	13A	116	40	43	8	2	152	64
Fr. 25.02.40 till 13.03.40	7A	242	82	101	37	15	192	61
	13A	58	18	54	9	7	102	29

46 in Peterhof and no.47 in Pusjkin. When first put into operation, lacking needed tools, supplies and spare-parts, they managed to repair only one tank every 4-5 days. But as they became fully up and running, repair efficiency increased to one tank per day.

The weakest point of the Soviet tank forces' operation in the war with Finland was very probably the lack of towing resources. Not only the tank battalions but even certain tank brigades were without tractors that had the capacity to tow disabled tanks from the battlefield. Tractors that were requisitioned from civilian owners proved to have engines with insufficient horsepower and many of them were in need of repair or not even repairable. As regards the special tow-vehicle, the "Kommintern" – they were few in number. Over the course of the war, a new type of tow-vehicle, the "Vorosjilovet" which had just gone into production, was increasingly delivered to the front. They distinguished themselves under battle conditions and were much praised by the repair units. In the main, however, it was still the tanks themselves that carried out the task of towing disabled tanks from the battlefield. On December 25, the 7th Army organized a towing company directly attached to the army that had 16 tractors at its disposal. Up until March 1, this company towed 196 BT's, 410 T-26's, 44 T-37/38's, 27 T-27's, 6 BA-6's, and 26 disabled examples of the T-20. In addition, 80 T-26's, 30 BT's, and 18 T-37's were dragged out of rivers and swamps.

During the severe cold of 1939-40, great quantities of fuel were used to keep the tanks warm. Therefore, units of the 7th and 13th Armies came to use a heating system based on the tank brigades' experience. Tanks were placed in specially dug out half-shelters and covered with a tarp or a log roof – then a little fire would be kept burning under the tanks' armored-flooring. The result was that, no matter the cold, engines were easy to start. By the end of January 1940, specially designed engine-warmers began to arrive that were notably less risky than a fire burning under the floor of a tank.

A type T-28 tank from the 90th Tank Battalion, 20th Heavy Tank Brigade that was destroyed during battle on December 18, 1939, and abandoned in enemy territory. The picture was taken on Feb. 2, 1940. (ASKM)

A Finnish Vickers that was destroyed in battle on Feb 26, 1940 in the Honkaniemi area. Farthest back is a T-28 from the 20th Heavy Tank Brigade. (ASKM)

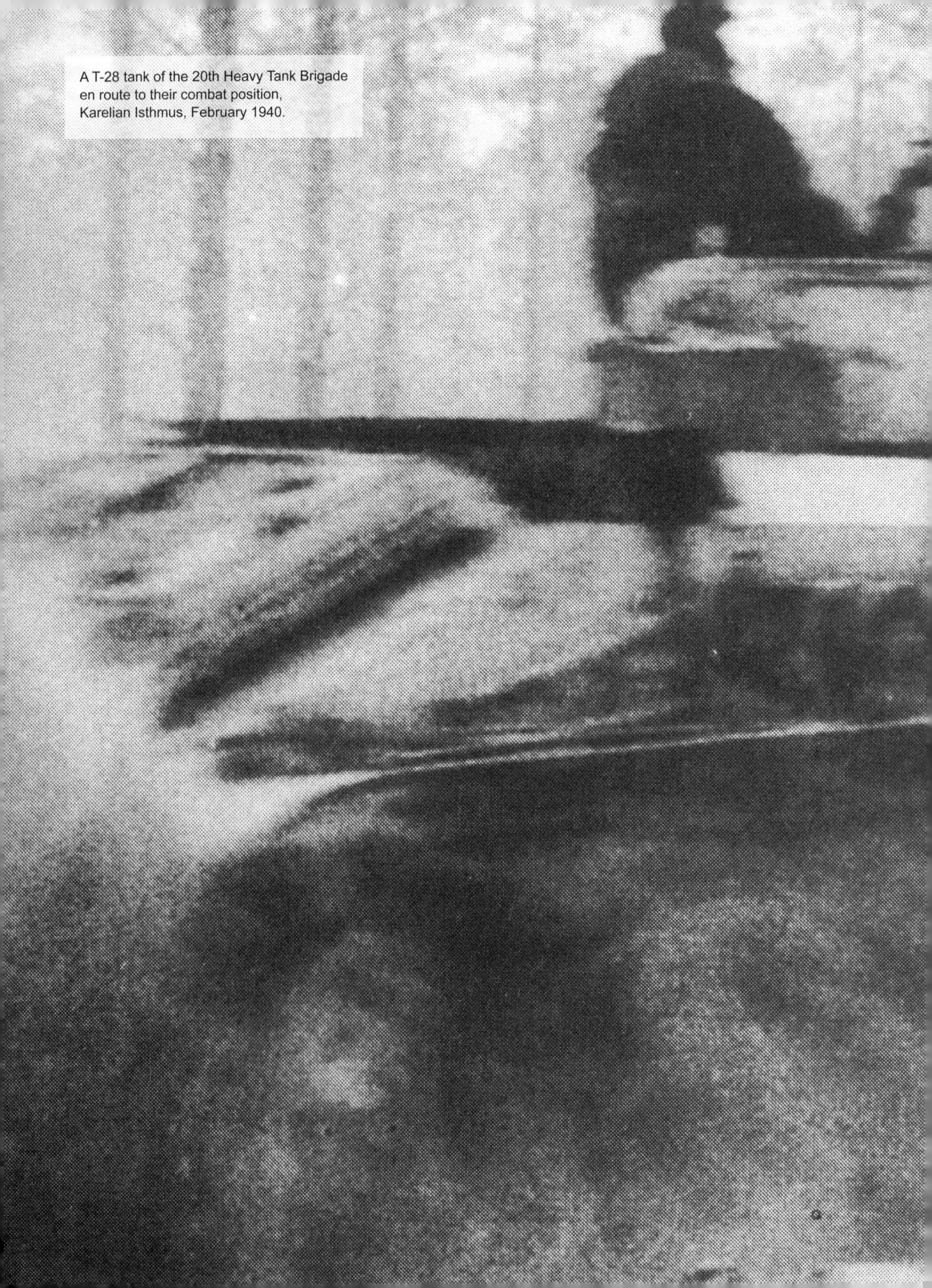

A T-28 tank of the 20th Heavy Tank Brigade en route to their combat position, Karelian Isthmus, February 1940.

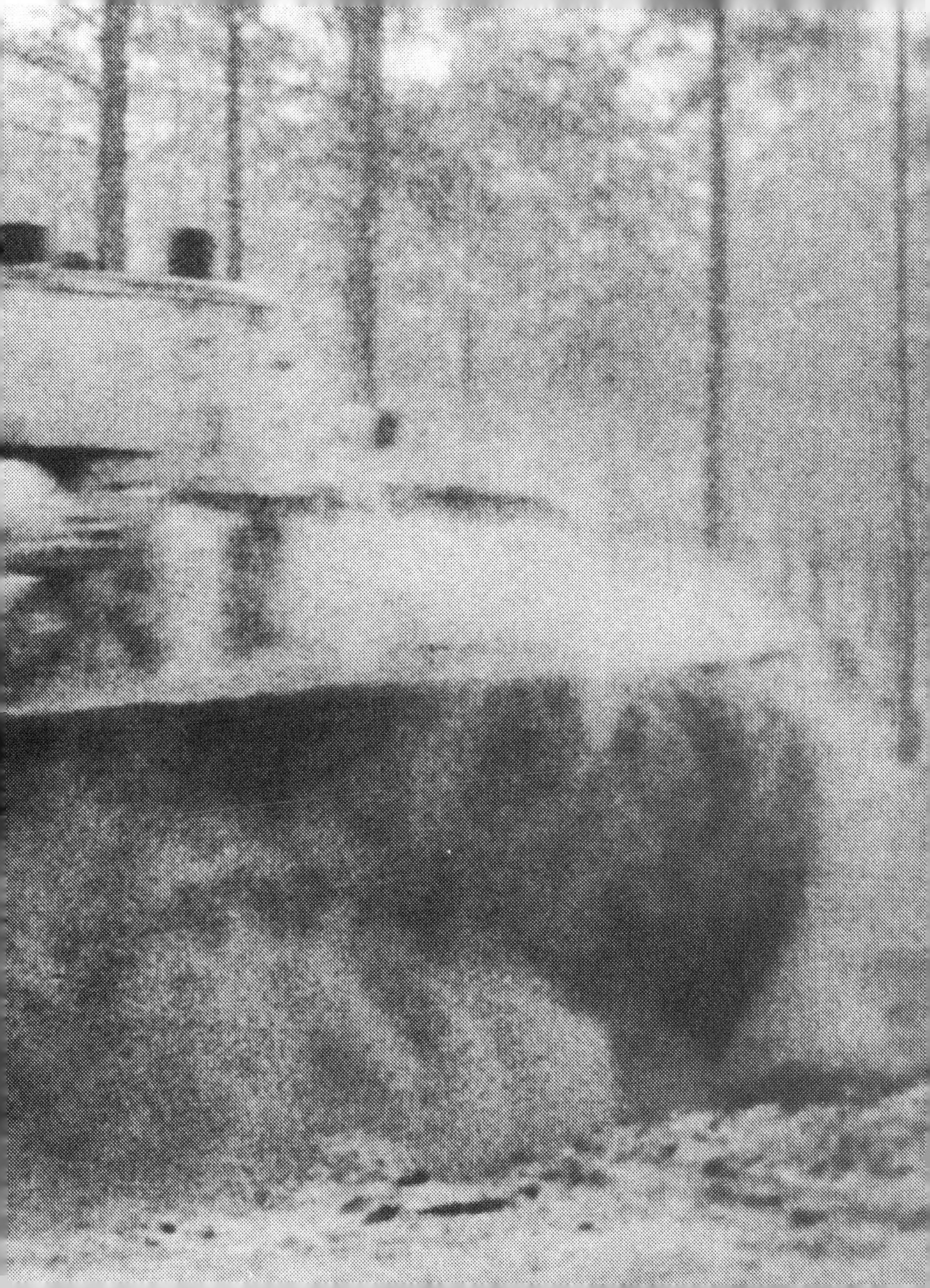

A T-26, model 1939, on its way to a battle site, Karelian Isthmus, Feb. 1940. The tank has been repainted white and on the side of the turret can be seen the tactical marking "00." Fastened on the stern is a bundle of logs and shrubs that can be laid out to cross anti-tank moats. (ASKM)

A T-26, model 1939, en route to battle, Karelian Isthmus, Feb. 1940. The vehicle is painted over in white, and wood is bundled on its left side to get over anti-tank moats. (ASKM)

3:2 Tank forces in battle on the Karelian Isthmus

Below is a brief overview of the armored forces contained in the warring armies from November 30, 1939 through March 13, 1940. The author has, insofar as possible, tried to provide the following information: The commanders and commissioners' names, the units' various structures, the number of combat vehicles, a résumé of the course of war with a number of interesting episodes from the fighting, information about losses and the total number of combatants who were awarded commendations and/or medals. However, far from all the information was saved in archive documents – This simply isn't possible – Consequently, in a series of statistical tables, the information provided is incomplete. If there doesn't appear a breakdown between "battle losses" and "technical losses," then under the heading "losses" only those losses that occurred in battle are cited.

The 10th tank corps

The commanding officer was Brigade Commander Versjinin. At the beginning of the war this corps was made up of the 1st and 13th Light-Tank Brigades, plus the 15th Machine Gun Brigade, and was manned with well-trained troops. The tanks were badly worn by the long marches – in total, over 800 kilometers –made in September-October to the Estonian and Latvian borders, and then to the Karelian Isthmus in November.

Over the first days of battle, successive attempts to use the corps solely to breakthrough the defence and carry out quick attacks behind the Finnish lines were unsuccessful, and at the close of December 1939, the corps was disbanded and, from there on out, it functioned as a brigade. The corps' commanding officer was appointed commander of the 7th Army's armored-car forces.

The 1st light tank brigade

The commanding officer was Brigade Commander V. Ivanov. At the start of the war, it consisted of the 1st, 4th, 8th and 9th Tank Battalions, the 202nd Reconnaissance Battalion, the 167th Mobile Rifle Battalion, the 314th Motor Vehicle Transportation Battalion, the 53rd Special Liaison Company, the 6th Combat-Supply Company, the 37th Engineer Company, the 313th Medicine and Medical Care Company, as well as the 52nd Company from the tank reserves – in all, 178 tanks and 23 armored-vehicles.

During the first days of battle, the brigade operated within the 10th Tank Corps. Thereafter, throughout January 1940, its mission was to carry out combat training and equipment repair necessary to the brigade. At the start of February, it was assigned to the 10th Rifle Corp, where its activities were concentrated in the Melola district until February 5, when it received orders to take the heavily fortified heights of "Grusja" and 38.2. From February 5-8, intensive reconnaissance was carried out, participating infantry units were educated about being transported in "Solotov" armored sleds, and underwent training exercises in getting through anti-tank obstacles,

Nevertheless, an attack launched on February 9 proved fruitless – it became all too apparent that the Finn's combat installations on height 38.2 were not destroyed and that the surrounding terrain contained closely-spaced obstacles of felled trees, earth walls, and trenches, along with an incredible amount of craters – the result of bombs and heavy grenades. Thus, it was clear that a successful assault of height 38.2 could only come about through a main input of infantry, supported by tanks firing from set positions – and on February 14-15, this reasoning was carried out..

Beginning February 21, the 1st Tank Brigade became a part of the 7th Army's reserve, and on February 37 it was assigned to the 34th Rifle Corps in order take part in a joint action to drive the enemy into retreat and seize Viborg. In carrying out this mission, the brigade took

TABLE 3. INFORMATION REGARDING THE 1ST TANK BRIGADE FROM NOVEMBER 30, 1939 UNTIL MARCH 13, 1940.

Type of armored vehicle	In place at the start of war	New production recvd during the war	losses – Due to artillery fire	mines	fire	Sunk in water	Tech. causes	restored
BT-7	-	112	31	31	23	8	8	51
BT-7A	6	-	4	2	-	-	-	6
BT-5	83	22	18	19	2	3	74	32
BT-2	82	16	8	8	4	2	68	11
T-26	7	1	-	-	2	-	4	-
BA-10	18	6	3	-	-	-	3	6
BA-20	5	-	-	1	-	-	3	4
ChT-133	-	5	-	-	-	-	-	-

A "Komintern" evacuating a destroyed tank, Karelian Isthmus, Feb. 1940. (CAFM)

Säiniö under battle on February 29, and on March 3, it began engaging in battles around Temmäsuo, which continued on until the war's end.

The conduct of the tank crews was diligent and courageous – but at the same time, the infantry of the 91st Rifle Division not only refused to go on attack but sometimes failed to even open fire. And infantry soldiers being transported on tanks fled at the first sign of enemy fire. Therefore, at the request of the tank crews, the chief of staff for 91st Rifle Division, on the night of March 12-13, assembled a small group of soldiers beside the tanks. These soldiers, who that night would advance with the tanks and secure a new frontline, were generously rewarded with "orders" (special Soviet commendations) with the aim of boosting combat morale.

During combat, BT-7A type tanks (with 76 mm guns) particularly distinguished themselves. They were joined to a special artillery group and were used to neutralize Finnish firing positions and artillery batteries.

Throughout the war, the weakest point in the 1st Tank Brigade was the total absence of towing resources. Not until the end February did they get a "Kommintern" type tractor, a "Vorosjilovets" and two TiTZS-65's.

Losses taken during the entire conflict: 177 killed, 519 wounded and 67 missing in action.

The 13th light tank brigade

The commanding officer was Brigade Commander V. Baranov. At the war's start, the brigade consisted of the 6th, 9th, 13th, and 15th Tank Battalions, the 205th Reconnaissance Battalion, the 158th Mobile Rifle and Motor Vehicle Transportation Battalion, and the 8th Combat Supply Company – In total, there were 256 tanks. The 13th Tank Brigade, then a part of the 10th Tank Corps, was sent into battle on December 1 and advanced in the direction of Kiviniemi, which was taken on December 5. In the course of this advance, the brigade fought through 7 anti-tank trenches and 17 rows of stone anti-tank obstacles

On December 16, after a series of marches, the brigade concentrated its activities to Peinola and the mission of expanding the 123rd Rifle Division's breakthrough, going on the offensive towards Lähde and the Kämärä railway station, along with seizing the Tali station.

The battalions got underway on December 17 but didn't succeed in breaking through the lines and the entire brigade came to a halt. At 13:00 hours on December 18, the brigade found itself at the location it had started from and became the target of heavy artillery fire, resulting in two tanks being set ablaze and eight tanks being hit with grenades. Thereafter, the brigade retreated to the Bobjino district – away from the front. Here, from December 23, 1939 to February 13, 1940, the brigade carried on intensive preparation for battle. Among other improvements, studs were set into the track-feet of BT tanks to better their ability to move forward and maneuver under winter conditions. Shooting apart stone and concrete anti-tank obstacles was also practiced – results revealed that a 45 mm tank grenade totally destroyed such obstacles. With this knowledge in hand, tank crews began to be trained in the methods these anti-tank obstacles, which they frequently encountered on maneuvers, could be crushed and otherwise destroyed and this learning came to be carried out by tank units in future combat situations. The brigades "rest" period coincided with a period of extreme cold, heavily taxing engine resources and large quantities of fuel just to keep combat vehicles at the ready. At the initiative of soldiers and officers, different types of earth shelters were built to help keep tanks relatively warm.

From February 13 to March 13, the brigade participated in expanding the breach in the Finnish main line of defence, "the Mannerheim Line," both as a complete brigade and as individual battalions.

On February 14, the brigade's tanks began to engage in battles for Lähde, which was quickly occupied despite persistent resistance. During this assault, tanks equipped with flame-throwers proved their worth by annihilating the forces of their opponent in infantry trenches and fox-holes.

By the evening of February 15, battalions with the 13th Tank Brigade had reached the Kämärär railway station, which was taken the following day after intense fighting.

During the battle for Kärämä, approximately 800 enemy soldiers fell and 80 were taken captive – 8 "Renault" type tanks, devoid of weaponry, were captured, and 12 field guns, 16 machine guns and 12 earth shelters were destroyed. The brigade's losses mounted to 10 tanks

Over the following days, the tank crews took control of the Pero railway station. On March 5, Mannikala was occupied

Befälhavaren för 13:e lätta stridsvagnsbrigaden V. Varanov (på fotot från 1945 hade han generallöjtnants grad). *(RGK-FAD)*

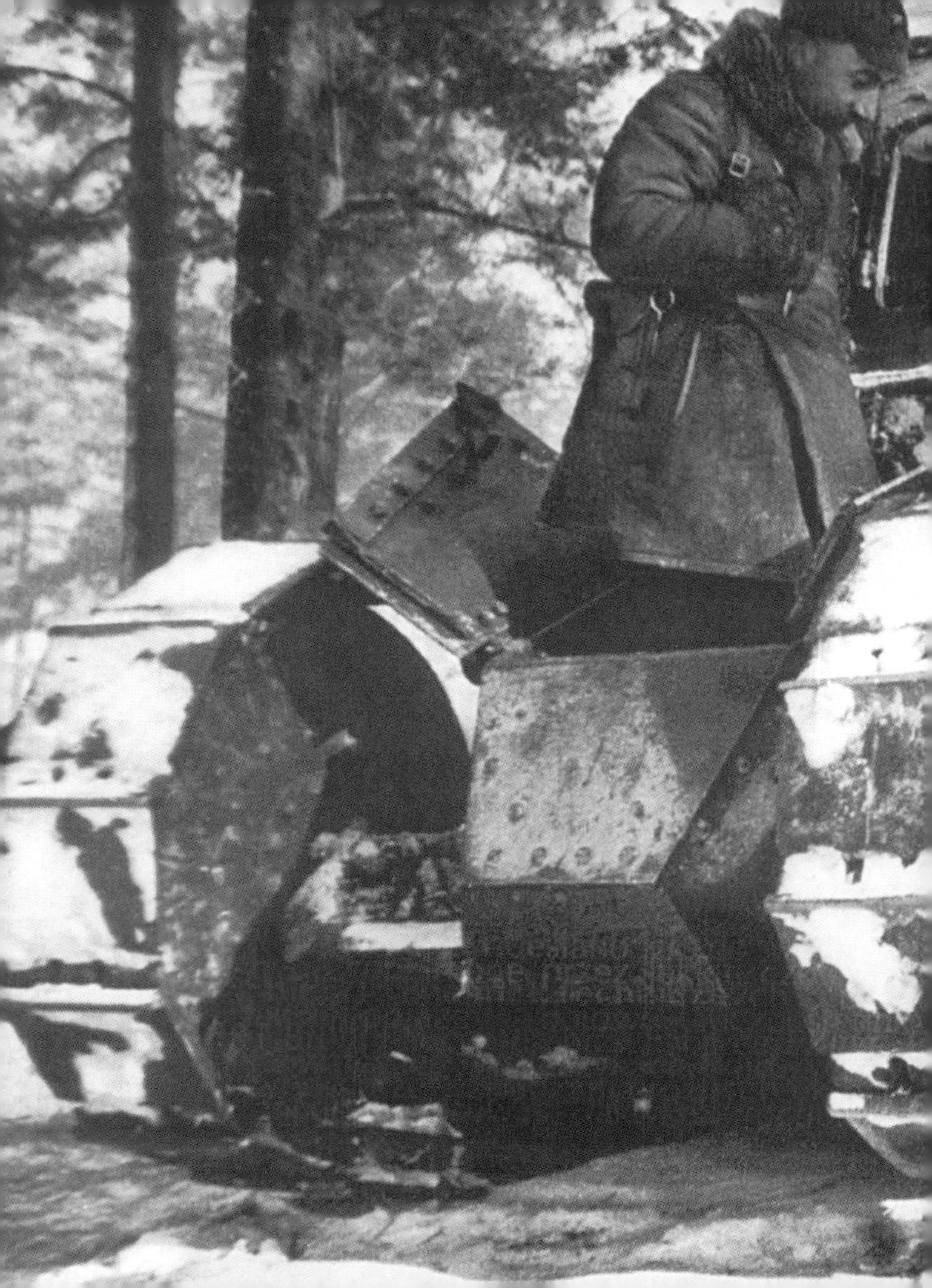

Russian soldiers inspect a abandoned Finnish Renault FT light tank at Pero railwaystation in February 1940.

TABLE 4. INFORMATION REGARDING THE 13TH TANK BRIGADE FROM NOVEMBER 30, 1939 UNTIL MARCH 13, 1940					
Type of armored vehicle	In place vehicles at the war's start	New vehicles received during the war	Losses		
			artillery fire	*mines*	*fire*
BT-7	246	67	122	63	52
BT-2	-	2	-	-	-
T-26	10	5	2	1	2

after intense fighting – so too Repola on March 10, and before the war ended, Nurmilampi was also taken.

Throughout the entire war, all the brigade's necessities were transported to the front by tanks because vehicles with only wheels simply couldn't. Cargo was secured to the tanks and a truck coupled to the back and then the tank moved off. At the beginning of hostilities, the 13th Tank Brigade had, in all, two tractors of the "Kommintern" type that couldn't manage the task of towing disabled tanks. Consequently, disabled tanks had to be towed by other tanks.

Losses during the entire war totalled 234 killed, 484 wounded and 23 missing in action.

By decree of the President of the Highest Soviet for the USSR, the 13th Light Tank Brigade was awarded the "Order of the Red Banner of Combat." for its contribution to battles on the Karelian Isthmus,

The 15th machine gun brigade

The commanding officer was Colonel Gavrilov, and the commissioner was Regimental Commissioner Malusjin. At the beginning of the war, this brigade was a part of the 10th Tank Corps and consisted of the 153rd, the 158th, and the 167th Machine Gun Battalions and had at its disposal 27 BA-10's, 7 BA-20's and 24 "Komsomolets" tow-vehicles. The brigade worked in close co-operation with the 1st and 13th Tank Brigades. Over the course of fighting, they were reinforced by the addition of three BA-20's and 19 BA-10's. Losses during the war mounted to three BA-10's, one BA-20 and five "Komsomolets."

The 20th heavy-tank brigade

The commanding officer was Brigade Commander Borzilov, and its commissioner was Regimental Commissioner Kulik. At the beginning of the war, the brigade consisted of the 90th and 95th Tank Battalions, the 256th Repair and Maintenance Battalion, the 301st Motor Vehicle Transportation Battalion; and the 215th Reconnaissance Company, the 302nd Chemical Company,

Befälhavaren för 20:e tunga stridsvagnsbrigaden brigadchef P. Borzilov. Stupade hösten 1941. *(RGKFAD)*

the 57th Liaison Company, the 38th Engineer Company, the 45th Anti-aircraft Company, and the 65th Company from the Armored Vehicle Reserve, along with the 7th Special Company (for radio-controlled tanks) – in all, 2,926 men, 145 tanks, 20 armored vehicles, 20 passenger cars, 378 trucks and 95 specialized vehicles, 96 motor cycles and four tractors.

Over the first days of battle, the Brigade worked together with the 19th Rifle Division, but on December 17, it was transferred to the 50th Rifle Corps. Up until February 17, it participated in battles in the Summa-Hottinen district, and thereafter in the districts of Honkaniemi, Pero and Tali. Brigade personnel combat-casualties totalled 169 killed, 338 wounded and 57 missing in action. Included among the 613 commendations awarded the brigade's personnel were: 21 "Hero of the Soviet Union," 14 "Order of Lenin," 97 "Order of the Red Banner for Combat," 189 "Order of the Red Star," and 292 medals "for bravery" and "for service in combat."

By decree of the President of the Highest Soviet in the USSR, the 20th Tank Brigade was awarded the "Order of the Red Banner for Combat" for its battle contributions on the Karelian Isthmus. (More details about the battles of the 20th Heavy-Tank Brigade, and about the input of T-28's, in the Soviet-Finnish War can be read in the publication "Frontillustration" No. 4, year 2000: "Multi-turret tanks in the RKKA/Red Army/ T-28 and T-29")

The 29th light tank brigade

The Commanding officer was Brigade Commander Krivosjen and its commissioner was Regimental

TABLE 5. INFORMATION REGARDING THE 20TH HEAVY TANK BRIGADE FROM NOVEMBER 30, 1939 UNTIL MARCH 13, 1940.

Type of armored vehicle	In place at war's start	New tanks, etc. Rcvd Over war	Losses — Due to Artly. fire	mines	fire	Sunk in water	Lost w/o trace (MIA)	Tech cause	Total losses	Repaired during war	Non-restorable losses
T-28	105	67	155	77	30	21	2	197	482	371	32
T-26	11	-	1	1	1	-	-	10	13	14	-
BT-5	8	-	2	1	-	4	-	}22	}32	}19	}2
BT-7	21	-	1	1	1	-					
BA-6	5	-	-	-	-	-	-	-	-	-	-
BA-20	15	-	-	-	-	-	-	-	-	-	-

Commissioner Illarionov. The brigade arrived from Brest on February 27, and at that time consisted of the 165th, 168th, 170th and the 172nd Tank Battalions, the 216th Reconnaissance Company and the 66th Engineer Company – with a total of 256 T-26 tanks. Until March 12, the tank crews were fully occupied with combat training where, among other things, they learned a great deal about bunkers and conducted shooting exercises.

At 3 A.M., March 12, the brigade received orders to provide support to the 34th Rifle Corps in the assault of Viborg. Inasmuch as the access roads to the city were heavily mined, the tanks gave fire-cover from more-or-less fixed positions, destroying two anti-tank guns, a bunker and ten firing installations. A tank crew under the command of Seargent Katatjov was particularly heroic – it succeeded in advancing to within 150 meters of the Finnish emplacements and, by making excellent use of its main gun, blew to bits a bunker that was preventing the infantry from advancing.

At the war's end – 12 noon, March 13 – the brigade's tanks were the first to enter Viborg and occupy the north, northeast and western suburbs of the city. The Brigade's losses during the fighting mounted to five men killed and 18 wounded; nine tanks were hit.

Befälhavaren för 29:e lätta stridsvagnsbrigaden S. Krivosjejn (på fotot från 1945 har han generallöjtnants grad). (RGKFAD)

The 35th light tank brigade

The commanding officer was Colonel Kosjuba and its commissioner was Regimental Commissioner Jarosj. On November 30, the brigade consisted of the 105th, 108th and 112th Tank Battalions, the 230th Reconnaissance Battalion, the 37th Supply Company, and the 61st Engineer Company – in total, 2,716 men, 146 tanks, one tow-vehicle, 20 armored vehicles, 403 trucks, and 124 specialized vehicles, along with 9 tractors. Earlier in November, before the outbreak of war, the brigade's 111th Battalion was transferred to the front line in the 8th Army's sector.

Combat vehicles were in good running order but, as with other units, the brigade had insufficient access to repair resources. In addition, the tractors were badly worn and their number short of satisfactory.

During the first days of fighting, the brigade took active part in the advance towards Kiviniemi, and thereafter was assigned to the Hottinen and height 65.5 district. Towards the end of December, the brigade's tanks attacked the enemy in support of the 123rd and 138th Rifle Divisions, suffering heavy losses. After which, it was withdrawn to the reserves. In January,

Befälhavaren för 35:e lätta stridsvagnsbrigaden V. Kasjuba (på fotot från 1941 har han generalmajors rang). (RGKFAD)

Finnish soldiers towing a Bofors 3,7cm AT gun thru the streets of Vyborg in March 1940. In the background one can see the towns Lycée.

Red Army soldiers check out a Vickers captured by the 4th Tank Company in the area of Honkaniemi, Feb, 1940. (CAFM)

A burning T-20 Komsomolets tractor on the Karelian Isthmus.

During the fi ghting in December, this T-26 were destroyed in front of the Mannerheim line.

A newly dug trenchline at Summa on the Karelian Isthmus in February 1940.

A destroyed T-26 early in December on the Karelian Isthmus. Most likely, it was stopped by anti-tank mines.

TABLE 6. INFORMTION REGARDING ARMORED VEHICLES IN THE 35ᵗʰ LIGHT TANK BRIGADE FROM NOVEMBER 30, 1939 UNTIL MARS 13, 1940.

Type of armored vehicle	In place at war's start	New vehicles received during the war	losses Due to artillery fire	mines	fire	Sunk in water	Restored during the war
T-26	136	137	51	53	33	8	70
ChT-26	10	-	2	3	5	-	2
ST-26	3	-	-	-	-	-	-
BA-10	10	-	-	-	-	-	-
BA-20	10	-	-	-	-	-	-

the tank crews carried out towing duties and repaired equipment, as well as participating in training exercises to improve co-operation among infantry, engineer units and artillery. On the basis of experience gained from earlier fighting, bundles of wood and branches were collected and then placed on sleds securely fastened to the back of a tank. The tactical plan was to use them to fill anti-tank trenches and the openings between stone and concrete obstacles. Acting on a suggestion made by the brigade's soldiers, a wooden bridge was constructed to span pits and trenches. The plan was to place the bridge on runners in front of a T-26 which could then push it along. The bridge construction, however, became very heavy and cumbersome, and hence, unsuitable for transport over hilly terrain.

At the beginning of the breakthrough of the central defence line "the Mannerheim Line" the brigade's tanks were divided, as battalions, among the 100ᵗʰ, 113ᵗʰ, and 123ʳᵈ Rifle Divisions where they remained active until the end of the war.

Disc-trawlers and bridge-deploying tanks were used during battle, but their impact was marginal. The towing and repair of disabled tanks was accomplished with great difficulty due to a lack of resources. The repair and maintenance battalion carried out its work in a decidedly "combined" way – It took parts from one tank and used them on another, and in this way, two disabled tanks were combined to make one that could be used in battle. At the beginning of the war, the brigade had only three "Kommintern" tow-vehicles – and those were in need of repair. In December, this tow-force was supplemented with three S-65 tractors, but they soon broke down. Thus, towing often required the help of T-28 tanks from the 20ᵗʰ Heavy Tank Brigade which lay close by.

Personnel losses during the war were 122 killed and 249 wounded. Commendations were awarded to 237 men, of whom 14 were decorated as "Heroes of the Soviet Union," 21 received the "Order of Lenin," 67 the "Order of the Red Star," 97 were awarded medals "for bravery" and 61 received medals for "service in battle."

The 39ᵗʰ light tank brigade

The commanding officer was Colonel D. Leljusjenko and the commissioner was Regimental Commissioner Solovjov. The brigade arrived at Leningrad's Military District at the end of November. On instruction of the general staff, the 100ᵗʰ and 97ᵗʰ Tank Battalions were withdrawn from the Brigade (to be transferred to the 9ᵗʰ Army), as well as the 198ᵗʰ Battalion (which became a part of the 1ˢᵗ Corps of the Finnish Peoples' Army). The remaining units were undermanned and under-equipped. At the start of hostilities, the brigade consisted of: the 85ᵗʰ Tank Battalion, the 232ⁿᵈ Reconnaissance Battalion, the 321ˢᵗ Motor Vehicle Transportation Battalion, and the 275ᵗʰ Repair and Maintenance Battalion, the 55ᵗʰ Engineer Company, the 23ʳᵈ Supply Company, the 99ᵗʰ Liaison Company, the 219ᵗʰ Medicine and Medical Care Company, along with the 78ᵗʰ Tank Company with the tank reserves – in all, 113 tanks, 15 armored vehicles, 179 cars and trucks, two mobile repair facilities (one "Type A" and one "Type B"), and one "Kommintern" tractor. In order to achieve a more powerful combat force, the reconnaissance battalion

Befälhavaren för 39:e lätta stridsvagnsbrigaden brigadchef Leljusjenko. (RGKFAD)

TABLE 7. INFORMATION REGARDING THE ARMORED VEHICLES IN THE 39TH LIGHT TANK BRIGADE FROM NOVEMBER 30, 1939 UNTIL MARCH 13, 1940.

Type of armored vehicle	In place at war's start	New vehicles received during the war	Losses – Due to artillery	mines	fire	Sunk in water
T-26	100	43	57	9	12	3
ChT-26	10	5	2	1	1	-
ST-26	-	1	-	-	-	-
Tow-vehicles .T-26	3	-	-	-	-	-
BA-20	15	8	-	-	-	-

was reinforced with a company from the tank reserves in the beginning of December, and at the initiative of the brigade's command, this unit was reorganized to form a tank battalion consisting of three companies (two tank companies and an armored vehicle company). In addition, on December 15, the 204th Chemical Tank Battalion was attached to the brigade and in February it was put directly under the brigade's command.

At the outbreak of hostilities, the 39th Tank Brigade was attached to the 50th Rifle Corps – and through December, they jointly fought in the Taipale district in the area of the Taipalenjoki river.

In the beginning of January, the brigade was withdrawn to the reserves and engaged in combat training and equipment repair. During this time, Colonel Leljusjenko organized training for soldiers in the reserves and in the various provision and supply units operating behind the front. Largely due to this foresight, the brigade never experienced a shortage of manpower in its tank crews for the remainder of the war.

In February, the 39th Tank Brigade engaged in battles in Muola-Oinila-Kyrelä sector and in the Llves district. In March, after an assault during which the brigade fought through a mined field with 12 timber barricades, two lines of granite stone obstacles and an anti-tank trench, Honkaniemi was taken. Thereafter, the offensive was expanded and by the war's end, units from the brigade had reached as far as Repola.

Losses during the war mounted to 65 killed, 117 wounded and 13 missing in action.

Of the 269 men who received war commendations, four were awarded "Hero of the Soviet Union." And by decree of the President of the Highest Soviet in the USSR, the 39th Light Tank Brigade was awarded the "Order of Lenin" for its contribution to the battles on the Karelian Isthmus.

The 40th light tank brigade

The commanding officer was Major Poljakov (promoted to Colonel in January 1940), and the commissioner was Regimental Commissioner Kolosjnikov. This Brigade was formed at the time of the "large education maneuver" as the reserve 2nd Armored Vehicle Regiment in the Leningrad Military District. The regiment, which originally contained two battalions of BT-type tanks, and two made up of T-26's, developed into a T-26 brigade, a changeover that created special problems related to re-training BT crews to the T-26. In addition, there were no sub-units that could have been formed into battalions for reconnaissance, transportation, and combat supply.

At the same time this unit was being formed into a brigade, its complement of personnel was augmented by an addition of manpower that approached 60 percent of its previous troop strength: These newcomers were drawn from the reserves, and the majority of them were called up by the recruiting authorities from reserve units that lacked training in the specific characteristics of tanks. In fact, many of these men had never actually served in the army. But thanks to the commander's energetic leadership, when the fighting began a combat ready unit had been created.

On November 30, the brigade consisted of the 155th, the 157th, the 160th and the 161st Tank Battalions, the 280th Repair and Maintenance Battalion, and the 336th Reconnaissance Company, the 307th Medicine and Medical Care Company and the 43rd Combat Supply Company – In total, there were 247 tanks, 24 armored

TABLE 8. INFORMATION REGARDING THE ARMORED VEHICLES IN THE 40TH TANK BRIGADE FROM NOVEMBER 30, 1939 UNTIL MARCH 13, 1940.

Type of armored vehicle	In place at war's start	New vehicles received during the war	Losses – Due to artillery fire	mines	fire	Sunk in water	Those that could not be repaired	Those that were repaired
T-26	201	76	69	58	46	7	65	74
БТ	34	-	5	3	4	-	4	-
ХТ-26	8	5	3	4	2	-	1	4
СТ-26	4	-	-	-	-	-	-	-
БА-20	6	-	-	-	-	-	-	-
БА-10	18	-	-	-	-	-	-	-

vehicles, 24 passenger cars, 262 trucks, 34 specialized vehicles and 41 tractors. The combat vehicles were in satisfactory running order, even though many tanks were dated models – BT-2's and BT-5's, and two-turreted T-26's.

A dearth of repair facilities heavily affected the brigade – there was only one "B-type" and six "A-type" mobile repair facilities. Of the 41 tractors requisitioned from civilian owners, 31 broke down after a week. At the beginning of the war, the brigade was placed at the disposal of the 19th Rifle Corps and divided, as battalions, among the rifle divisions. Enemy opposition was weak during the early days of the war – but despite this – the infantry lagged behind the tanks and, without the support of the tanks and intimidated by the deep forest around them, they would stop and declined to engage in any offensive action. Certain infantry commanders used the tanks assigned to them for personal concerns rather than combat missions. For example, the commander of the 274th Rifle Regiment employed them to escort kitchen equipment and as protection for the regimental bath.

Beginning December 6, intense battles were fought in an attempt to break through the central defence line in the Väisänen-Muola-Oinila district. This fighting raged on until December 29, but without anything having been achieved. The infantry followed along with the tanks – so long as the Finns didn't open fire. When they were subjected to enemy fire they would take instant cover on the ground and, for all practical purposes, it was impossible to get them to move. In the assault on Muola, for example, the tanks forced their way into to the town on five separate occasions, but each time the infantry failed to support them and they withdrew to their original starting point. During the assault of Oinila, they twice entered the community and the infantry, in fact, took over the Finnish trenches and blinds, but when they were fired upon, they retreated to their original positions.

During this period of combat, make-shift bridges constructed of timber were mounted on tanks along with bundles of tree branches to help get by anti-tank obstacles. But in very hilly terrain these fixes were less than effective.

As of December 29, the brigade had lost 86 tanks and was withdrawn from the front, where, over the months of January and February, they spent their time on restoring equipment and improving their tank knowledge.

By decree of the President of the Highest Soviet in the USSR, the 40th Light Tank Brigade was awarded "The Order of the Red Banner for Combat" for its contribution to the battles on the Karelian Isthmus.

Tank units of the 28th rifle corps

The corps, which was formed on February 29, consisted of the 43rd and 70th Rifle Divisions, and the 86th and 173rd Motorized Rifle Divisions, and was assigned the mission of crossing the Gulf of Finland during the night of March 3-4 and in this way approach the enemy forces defending Viborg from the rear. Starting out on March 3, the tightly assembled corps quickly crossed iced-over Gulf of Finland and by March 5, it was able to firmly secure a coastal base. During the following days, it engaged in intense fighting with the objective of expanding this beachhead.

The corps' complement of tank units included the 28th Tank Regiment and the 361st Tank Battalion out of the 70th Division, the 62nd Tank Regiment from the 86th Division and the 22nd Tank Regiment out of the 173rd Division.

A type ChT-130 tank out of the 210th Special Chemical Battalion carrying out flamethrowing, Karelian Isthmus, Feb. 1940. (RGAKFD)

BT-5 and BT-7 tanks abandoned at the place where the 34th Light Tank Brigades was crushed, 8th Army Zone, south Lemetti, Feb.1940. (ASKM)

T-26 models with different modifications (1933 tanks with circular, rail-like antennas, anti-aircraft machine guns and spot lights for night combat, and the 1933 models with double machine gun turrets), from the 35th Light Tank Brigade, at the front, Feb. 1940. (CAFM)

The 22nd tank regiment
The commanding officer was Major Malusjev, and the commissioner was Political Commander Gontjarov. It arrived at the front in February with a complement of seventy-six T-26's, five SNT-130's, and two BA-20's. Under battle, it lost 11 tanks.

The 28th tank regiment
The commanding officer was Major Skornjakov. It arrived at the front in February with a complement of 126 T-26 tanks. During battle, it lost 16 tanks, six of which were not repairable. Of the 105 regimental personnel awarded with "orders" and medals, four were honoured as "Heroes of the Soviet Union."

The 62nd tank regiment
The commanding officer was Major Vasiljev. It arrived from the city of Grudek-Jagellonskij in Kiev's Military District in February with a complement of 76 T-26's (15 were of the old two turret model) and seven SNT-26's. During the course of combat, its personnel losses mounted to 53 killed, 65 wounded, and five drowned – vehicle losses mounted to 53 (of which 28 were non-repairable).

The 63rd tank regiment
The commanding officer was Major Pankov, and Usatjev was the commissioner. It arrived from Zjitomir in Kiev's Military District on February 29 with a complement of 76 T-26's. During battle, personnel losses mounted to six killed, 11 wounded, and five drowned – regarding tank losses: five were damaged by gun fire, and six sunk in water.

The 14th special tank battalion
On February 14, it had 32 T-38 tanks and eight T-37's.

The 1st special tank battalion
The commanding officer was Lieutenant Vodopjan. The battalion was formed in Charkov's Military District and arrived on the Karelian Isthmus December 11, 1939 with a complement of 54 T-38 tanks. The battalion was attached to the 136th Rifle Division. In combat, the tanks were used to provide mobile fire support on the flanks and in the gaps between attacking infantry units. In short, its combat duties varied with the situation. In addition, they defended the division's command headquarters, transported wounded from the battlefield and acted as ammunition carriers. Personnel losses: three wounded –

"Komsomolets" type armoured tow vehicle on a street in Viborg, Mar. 13 1940. (ASKM)

tank losses: one tank set ablaze, two damaged by gun fire, and three disabled due to technical causes.

The 38th tank battalion
Arrived at the front on December 20 equipped with T-37 type tanks. Up-to-date losses recorded on February 25 mounted to 18 vehicles, four due to artillery fire, the rest were disabled due to technical causes.

The 41st special tank battalion
On February 14, it had 54 T-37/38's.

The 81st special tank battalion
On February 14, it had 37 T-37/38's.

The 204th special chemical tank battalion
Arrived from Kiev's Military District on November 25, 1939 with a complement of 20 SNT-26's and 30 SNT-130's. Participated in battle from November 30 to December 25 together with the 70th Rifle Division – thereafter, attached to the 23rd Rifle Corps and worked in co-operation this rifle division until the war's end.

The battalion's personnel losses throughout the war mounted to 23 killed, 33 wounded, one frozen to death and two missing in action.

Tank losses were as follows: 32 due to artillery fire and mines, 10 of which were non-repairable.

Commendations: one "Hero of the Soviet Union," 13 "Order of the Red Star," eight "Order of Lenin," five "Order of the Red Banner for Combat," one "Order of Exceptional Honor," 19 medals "for bravery" and three "for service in combat."

The 210th special chemical tank battalion
The commanding officer was Captain Murasjov, and the military commissioner was Political Commander Sjarandin. Attached to the 24th Rifle Division at the beginning of the war, the battalion had seven T-26 type tanks and 28 SNT-130's. Over the period December 7-15, the battalion lost 15 vehicles in the Väisä area. Thereafter, it was converted to complete the make up of a material supply unit attached to the 50th Rifle Corps. It continued to operate in this capacity until the end of the war.

The 217th special tank battalion (experimental tanks)
The commanding officer was Lieutenant Lebedev. On December 10, the battalion was placed at the disposal of the 20th Heavy-Tank Brigade. On December 17, the

Prototype of a model SMK tank disabled and abandoned by its crew inside the Finnish front line near Summa on the Karelian Isthmus, Dec. 1939. (Tank Museum)

The commander and a group of soldiers from the 210th Special Chemical Tank Battalion, who were awarded with "orders" and medals for their combat contribution on the Karelian Isthmus, Mar. 1940. The battalion commander, Captain Murasjov, is in the middle of the first row. (ASKM)

Amored-Train no. 16 in the Viborg area, Mar. 1940. Journalists reporting on the front stand in the foreground. (CAFM)

battalion's companies began to work in co-operation with the brigades battalions: The 1st Company supported the 123rd Rifle Division's infantry with tanks controlled by manned levers (manual steering), and then sent in three radio-controlled groups/teams. But the radio-controlled tanks couldn't get by the anti-tank obstacles, and having lost one tank, the company changed back to manual steering. The 2nd and 3rd Companies set out five radio-controlled groups without having carried out preliminary reconnaissance of the terrain. The radio-controlled tanks were trailed by the 20th Heavy Tank Brigade. Once into the anti-tank obstacles, they encountered heavy artillery fire, and after losing five radio-controlled tanks, the companies withdrew. Thereafter, the 2nd and 3rd companies were attached to the 650th Rifle Division and provided support to the infantry with tanks controlled by manned levers. From December 21, 1939 to February 8, 1940, the battalion was fully occupied with evacuating and repairing disabled tanks and other tasks related to combat readiness.

On February 10, the brigade received orders from the commander of the 7th Army's armoured car and tank forces to ready three radio-controlled tanks to engage in setting explosives to demolish concrete bunkers in the Hottinen area. The tanks were loaded with explosive material and, after reconnoitring the direction of attack towards the target, one the tanks was set off in the direction of bunker (DOT) no.35. But, as it happened, it was hit and exploded before reaching the target. Following this, two more radio-controlled tanks were exploded in the same way.

Between February 14-18, a company of radio-controlled tanks was used to clear away a path through a minefield, whereby 14 tanks were lost. On February 18, the battalion was transferred to the reserves and didn't take part in further battles. Total personnel losses for the entire period prior to this date: 14 killed and 16 wounded – Total tank losses: 42 taken out of action, six of which were totally destroyed, 21 were sent away for total restoration, and 15 were able to return to the battalion.

The 307th special tank brigade in the 80th rifle division

Arrived at the front on January 8 with a complement of 32 type T-26 tanks and four SNT-26's. During the fighting, the battalion was supplied with an additional ten T-26 tanks. Loss of personnel during the entire war mounted to five killed, and 19 wounded – total tank losses: four due to artillery fire, eight due to mines, and 20 due to technical causes.

The 315th special tank battalion

The commanding officer was Captain Jevtuchov. On November 30, the battalion had eight T-26 and 28 T-37 tanks. Losses for the entire war: three T-26's and one T-37 due to artillery, two T-26's and seven T-37's due to mines, one T-37 sunk in water, and one T-37 and three T-26's unable to function due to technical causes. Of these losses, two T-26's and eight T-37's were not repairable.

A very unusual picture from the Winter War – the T-27 light tank patrolling a road, 14th Army Zone, Mar. 1940. (ASKM)

A BA-10 armored car captured by the Finns, Varkaus, Feb. 1940. (E. Muikku)

Meeting the tank personnel who have returned from the front after war, Leningrad, Mar. 27, 1940. (ASKM)

The Finnish forward trenchline on the Karelian Isthmus in February 1940. Note the Armored shield in use in the trench.

109

Tanks from the 377th Special Tank Battalion leaving the front after terminated fighting, Karelian Isthmus, Mar. 1940. (ASKM)

The 317th special tank battalion in the 100th rifle division

Arrived from the city of Lida in the White Russian Military District in February 1940 with a complement of 12 T-26 tanks (six with 45 mm guns, one with two gun-turrets, the remaining with two machine gun-turrets), three ST-26's and 17 T-37/38's.

The 320th special tank battalion in the 14th rifle division

Arrived at the front on December 11. On February 16, the battalion had 16 T-26's and 17 T-37/38's.

The 350th special tank battalion in the 17th motorized rifle division:

Arrived at the front on January 20 with 19 BT-7's, four BT-5's and nine T-26's.

The 339th special tank battalion in the 90th rifle division.

The commanding officer was Lieutenant Kokka. Arrived at the front on February 29 with 12 T-26's, 20 T-37's, and two T-38's. War losses: six T-26's due to artillery fire, one T-37 due to mines, and eight T-37's due to technical causes.

The 355th special tank battalion in the 84th motorized rifle division:

Arrived at the front in February 1940 with 37 BT-7's and 12 SNT-130's. Participated in battle from February 16 to March 13 in the area of Pyhän-Perä, Ojala and Pero. When the Pero railway station was taken, two "Vickers" tanks, abandoned on the platform, were also captured (one had caught fire and one was missing its tracks) – and a "Renault."

Personnel losses: 11 killed and 22 wounded. Vehicle losses: three BT-7's and one SNT-130 due to artillery fire – Six BT-7's due to mines – nine BT-7's due to burning – five BT-7's had sunk in water, and seven BT-7's and nine SNT-130's became disabled due to technical causes.

TB-21 A BT-7 from an unknown tank unit getting over an obstacle somewhere on the Karelian Isthmus, winter 1940. (Tank Museum)

The 357th special tank battalion in the 11th rifle division

The commanding officer was Lieutenant Ivanovitj. On November 30, the battalion rolled over the border with ten T-26's and 20 T-38's. On December 2, a T-38 platoon was ordered to reconnoitre the railway station in Ino. When this mission was fully carried out and the platoon, in the process of making its way back, was about to attempt a difficult run over sheet ice and up a steep embankment, it suddenly came across an enemy force of almost battalion strength with artillery, which immediately set about trying to penetrate the tanks formation. The tanks returned fire and a battle ensued that lasted until the morning when the enemy decided to disengage its attack. Three T-38's were put out of action by artillery, four crew members were killed and one wounded. After this incident, the battalion was incorporated into 70th Rifle Division's force until the war's end.

The battalion's losses for the entire war mounted to 23 killed, 18 wounded and five frozen to death. Two T-38's and four T-26's were exploded by mines, four T-38's and 11 T-26's were lost to artillery fire, and four T-38's and 11 T-26's were disabled for technical causes.

The 327th special tank battalion in the 95th rifle division

Arrived at the front on January 25. On February 25, it had 13 T-26 tanks and one T-26 tow vehicle.

The 377th special tank battalion in the 97th rifle division

The commanding officer was Captain Sidorenko, and the commissioner was Political Commander Piletskij. The battalion arrived at the front on January 28 with a complement of 31 T-26's (whereof 11 had two turrets) and six SNT-26's. On March 13, the battalion had four T-37's and seven T-38's. Personnel losses during the war mounted to: six killed, four wounded and ten frozen to death. Tank losses totalled: five T-26's, and two SNT-26's – 13 T-26's and four SNT-26's became disabled due to technical causes.

The 391st special tank battalion in the 49th rifle division

The commanding officer was Captain Filipisjin, and the commissioner was Political Commander Nikolajev. It arrived at the front with 14 T-26 and 12 T-38 tanks, on

February 24, the brigade lost its entire supply unit and guarded the division's staff for the remainder of the war. Personnel losses: 3 killed and 11 wounded.

The 405th special tank battalion
Arrived at the front on January 26 with 39 T-26's and six SNT-26's. Losses during the war totalled: six T-26's due to artillery fire, two T-26's exploded by mines, six T-26's by fire and two T-26's and six SNT-26's were disabled due to technical causes. Of these losses, four T-26's could not be restored.

The 436th special tank battalion in the 138th rifle division
The commanding officer was Captain Makarov. When the war began, the battalion had seven T-26's and 15 T-37's. The battalion's tanks supported the division's forces in battle in the area of Papillo, Hottinen through December 13-18. Thereafter, it had the responsibility of guarding the division's command post, and through the period February 5-15 it supported the division's infantry in the Hottinen area, where the battalion lost its entire supply unit.

The 442nd special tank battalion in the 150th rifle division
The commanding officer was Captain Timosjenko. It arrived at the front on November 30 with nine, double-turreted machine gun T-26's and 19 T-38's.

The 445th special tank battalion in the 142nd rifle division
Arrived at the front on November 30 with nine T-26's, six T-37's and ten T-38's.

The 6th special intelligence battalion in the 5th rifle division
The commanding officer was Captain Soriejesov – the commissioner was Political Commander Jersjov. It arrived on the Karelian Isthmus from the White Russian Military District with ten BA-10's and participated in the fighting beginning January 28. Losses during the war totalled: 25 killed, seven wounded – and three BA-10's were disabled due to technical causes.

The 33rd special intelligence battalion
On March 9, the battalion had two T-27's and two SU-1-12 (a 76 mm regimental gun mounted on a GAZ-AAA truck).

The 62nd special intelligence battalion in the 52nd rifle division.
Arrived on Karelian Isthmus from the city of Pinsk in White Russia. Participated in battle beginning November 30, at which time it had seven BA-10's and three BA-3's.

The 69th special intelligence battalion in the 100th rifle division.
Arrived from the city of Lida in the White Russian Military District in February 1940, at which time it had two BA-3's and nine BA-10's.

The 100th special intelligence battalion in the 80th rifle division
Arrived at the front on January 9 with ten BA-10's.

Abandoned model BT-5 tank, belonging to the 34th Light Tank Brigade, middle south Lemetti, Feb. 1940. (Tank Museum)

Soviet soldiers looking over a captured Finnish tank, make Renault, in the area of the Pero railway station, Feb, 1940. Originally camouflage painted in three colors, but is now covered over with winter-white paint. (ASKM)

Tanks out of the 210th Special Chemical Tank Battalion (ChT-133's and one ChT-134) after terminated fighting. The one ChT-134 (with supplementary armoured plating) is the only tank with winter camouflage, Karelian Isthmus, Mar, 1940. (CAFM)

A destroyed T-26, model 1933, radio equipped and belonging to the 8th Army, Dec. 1939. (Tank Museum)

The 114th special intelligence battalion in the 84th motorized rifle division:

The commanding officer was Lieutenant Popov. It was formed out of the 4th Tank Regiment located in the city of Naro-Fominsk and had a complement of one BT-7, 16 BT-5's, four BA-10's and one D-8. It arrived at the front on January 30, 1940 and remained until the war's end. It suffered no losses.

The 175th special intelligence battalion in the 150th rifle division

Participated in battle beginning November 30, 1939 with ten BA-10's.

The 250th special amored car battalion

On March 5, it had 24 BA-10's, 3 BA-6's, 4 BA-20's, and !7 FAI-M's. It did not participate in battle.

The 8th special division for armored trains

The commanding officer was Major Karasik. It arrived on January 21 from the White Russian Military District with two armored trains (one light, no.16, and one heavy, no.21), one DTR armoured trolley, one BA-10zjd armored car and one BA-20zjd (the designation "zjd" indicates a vehicle that can run on rails). The division stood at the disposal of the 19th Rifle corps' commander. Beginning February 6, the armored trains were routinely sent to bombard Finnish installations in the vicinity of the Perkjävi railway station with its on-board artillery.

When the most vital defence sector in "the Mannerheim Line" had been broken through, and the rail section between Leipäsuo and Kämärä restored, the division then had the opportunity to support the 123rd Rifle Division's attacking infantry, which it continued to provide until March 2.

During the fighting for Viborg, March 6-12, the division supported units from the 27th Rifle Regiment as they battled enemy firing positions in the area of Ojalaand Kiesila. On March 8, the division was delagated a test model of the motorized armored coach, MBV-2, to test it out under war conditions. Beginning March 10, the MVB-2 was used to fire on infantry positions in the vicinity of the Liimatta railroad facilities, thus drawing a significant amount of artillery and grenade fire upon itself and away from the infantry, allowing the latter to more easily advance.

Over the period, February 7 to March 12, the armoured trains and the MVB-2 fired 1,677 rounds of 107 mm grenades and 5, 252 rounds of 76 mm grenades.

The special tank companies in the rifle regiments

The tank company in the 27th Rifle Regiment of the 7th Rifle Division – on January 26, had 17 T-26's – subsequently, 10 were lost in battle.

The tank company in the 257th Rifle Regiment of the 7th Rifle Division – on January 26, had seven T-26's – subsequently, one was lost in battle

- The tank company in the 300th Rifle Regiment of the 7th Rifle Division – on January 26, had 17 T-26's – subsequently, it lost 11 in battle.
- The tank company in the 77th Rifle Regiment of the 80th Rifle Division – on January 8, had 17 T-26's – subsequently, it lost 14 in battle.
- The tank company in the 153rd Rifle Regiment of the 80th Rifle Division – on January 8, had 17 T-26's – subsequently, it lost 11 in battle.
- The tank company in the 218th Rifle Regiment of the 80th Rifle Division – on January 8, had 17 T-26's – subsequently, it lost 5 in battle.

The finnish tank forces' battle activities

In October 1939, the 1st and 2nd Companies of the tank battalion were already being sent to the districts of Taipale, Kämärä, and Pero on the Karelian Isthmus. And since the "Renault" tanks were essentially worthless in combat, they were mainly used as armoured firing emplacements. In the fighting that followed, 30 of the 34 "Renaults" were lost.

At the beginning of hostilities, the tank crews of the 1st and 2nd Companies were assigned the responsibility of towing captured combat vehicles. The first captured tank was removed from the front on December 14, and by the middle of February, a total of 27 vehicles had been extricated from the battlefield. Of these, five proved to be in operation. In addition, a great number of assorted parts and equipment was removed from the permanently disabled vehicles. Among other successes, the Finns were able to tow two T-38 tanks that had been disabled in the Summa district. This task, however, took a great deal time – specifically, from Jan 29 to February 4.

Originally, the plan called for converting this captured equipment into six armored platoons, but this idea was set aside, and on February 13, the personnel of the 1st and 2nd Companies were withdrawn from the front

The 4th Armored Company. under the command of Lieutenant Heinonen, consisted of 118 men, 13 "Vickers" (of which 10 were equipped with Bofors 37 mm guns), five motorcycles, two passenger cars, and 13 trucks. The company arrived at the front on February 25 in the Honkaniemi district. The very next morning, it was assigned the mission of providing support to an infantry attack by the 23rd Infantry Division.

On the morning of February 26, 6:15 A.M., eight "Vickers" (with Bofors guns) set out for battle. Due to engine malfunctions, two vehicles remained in place and only six tanks reached the Soviet force's positions. The Finnish tank crews, however, had to contend with bad luck – the infantry didn't follow with the tanks and, due to poorly executed scouting, their "Vickers" came up against tanks from the Red Army's 35th Light Tank Brigade. According Finnish archive documents, the destiny of these "Vickers" was decided as follows:

One "Vickers" numbered R-648 was fired upon and hit by several Soviet tanks, and caught fire. The tank commander was wounded but was able to get back to the Finnish line. The three other crew members were killed. "Vickers" R-667 was fired upon and hit as it was passing the train tracks and then abandoned by its crew. This tank was able to be towed back, but it couldn't be restored to able service and consequently was picked apart. Two "Vickers" - R-664 and R-667 – were fired upon and hit and came to standstill. For short while, the crews continued to return fire from their fixed positions but eventually these "Vickers" were also abandoned. "Vickors" R-668 attempted to knock over a tree but became stuck. Only one crew member managed to return unscathed – the others were killed. "Vickers" R-668 was also fired upon and hit.

In the operation report turned in by the 35th Light Tank Brigade covering its activities on January 26, the course of this tank encounter is laconically described as follows: "Two tanks, of the type 'Vickers' with infantry, advanced to the 245th Rifle Regiments right flank but were hit with gunfire. Four 'Vickers' came to give the infantry assistance but were hit with gunfire from the company commander's three tanks that were out on a reconnaissance patrol."

An even shorter version is given in the "Journal over the events of the war" from the 35th brigade: "On February 26, the 112th Tank Battalion, together with units from the 123rd Rifle Division, came to the Honkaniemi district where the enemy invited stubborn opposition and several times went on counter-attack. Here, were encountered two tanks of type 'Renault' and six of type 'Vickers' – of these, one 'Renault' and three 'Vickers' came to be towed and left with the staff of the 7th Army."

What further destiny awaited these captured "Vickers" isn't entirely clear. It's only known that two 'Vickers' tanks are in exhibitions titled "The White-Finns total defeat" – one in Moscow and one in Leningrad. One of these tanks was in the custody of the 377th Special Tank Battalion and one (R-668) wound up on the proving grounds in Kubinka, where it had been tested in the spring-summer of 1940.

The remaining "Vickers" in the 4th Company took part in some further fighting. On February 17, two of them went on attack against Soviet positions in support of the 68th Infantry Regiment in the Pero district. On February 29, the tanks, R-672 and R-666, once again went on attack but this time it led to misfortune: They came into an area positioned for attack by the Soviet 20th Tank Brigade. In documentation submitted by the brigades 91st Battalion this episode is described in a single line: "On an attack near the Pero railway station, a kilometer northwest of Värakoski, two tanks of type 'Vickers' we were immediately hit." According to Finnish information, three of the eight crew members were killed and one was wounded.

After these battles, the company was drawn back to Viborg. This was the last battle for the "Vickers" in the Winter War. In total, the Finns lost eight tanks, seven of which were captured by the Red Army. One was towed to safety but couldn't be repaired and therefore was taken apart.

During the war, the armored-car, Landsverk, was a part of the cavalry brigade in the Taipale district but it was withdrawn from the front on December 26. One Finnish armored train participated in battles on the Karelian Isthmus, and another took part in the direction of Petrozavodsk. In both case, they were used for firing upon the enemy from fixed positions.

Despite losses, Finland's complement of tanks significantly increased during the course of the war as a result of vehicles being captured and transported to the city of Varkaus. Using the location of the mechanical fabricator A. Ahlstrom LTD as a base, tank repair shops were set up and 162 captured vehicles were successfully repaired – and ready to yet again be used in war. During 1940, the arsenal of Finnish armored forces was augmented with 34 T-26 tanks, two ChT-26's, four ChT-130's, two T-28's, 29 T-37's, 13 T-38's, 56 "Komsomolets" type tow-vehicles, ten armored vehicles type BA-6/BA-10, plus ten armored vehicles type FAI, FAI-M and BA-20, along with one D-8 and one BA-27M.

115

A Finnish type Vickers tank out of the 4th Tank Company rendered harmless in the area of Honkaniemi, Feb. 16, 1940. (ASKM)

A Finnish Renault-17 tank buried in earth where it's made use of as a protected firing emplacement, in the area of the Pero railway station, Feb. 1940. (ASKM)

3:3 The battles North of Ladoga

The course of battle in general

At the start of the war, the 8th Army under the leadership of Division Commander I. Chabarov (on December 16, Major General G. Sjtern assumed this command), consisted of the 56th Rifle Corps (made up of the 18th, 56th, and 168th Rifle Divisions), the 75th, 139th, and 155th Rifle Divisions, and the 34th Tank Brigade. The army's mission was to advance to the Tohmajärvi-Sordavala line within ten days, and thereafter break through the defence and attack the Finnish forces on the Karelian Isthmus from the rear, as well as to join up with the 7th Army. Opposing the 8th Army stood the IV Army Corps (commanded by General J. Heiskanen, and later General V. Hägglund) consisting of only two infantry divisions – the 12th and the 13th.

In the early going, the Soviet offensive developed successfully – after a week of combat its forces had advanced 70 kilometers into Finnish territory. Alarmed by this situation, the commander-and chief of the Finnish army, K. Mannerheim, ordered that reinforcements be sent to the 4th Corps. On December 5, Colonel P Talvela formed a unit made up of eight infantry battalions and one infantry regiment. Despite the small number of troops, Talvela's unit mounted a counterattack on December 12 and crushed the 139th Rifle Division in three days. Shortly thereafter in an adjacent area, the 75th Rifle Division experienced the same destiny. Both Soviet divisions suffered heavy losses and in this sector the front remained stabilized for the rest of the war. At same time these counter-attacks were taking place, the 4th Corps launched an offensive against the 8th Army's divisions on the left flank. Under pressure from the Finns, the 18th and 168th Rifle Divisions were forced to break off their offensive on December 19 and go on defence. From the end of December, 1939 to the beginning of January, 1940, the Finns made two advances – one in the direction of Sordavala, the other in the direction of Pitäranta. As a result, units of the 18th and 168th Rifle Divisions and 34th Tank Brigade wound up being surrounded in

A BA-20M armored car captured by Finnish troops, February 1940.

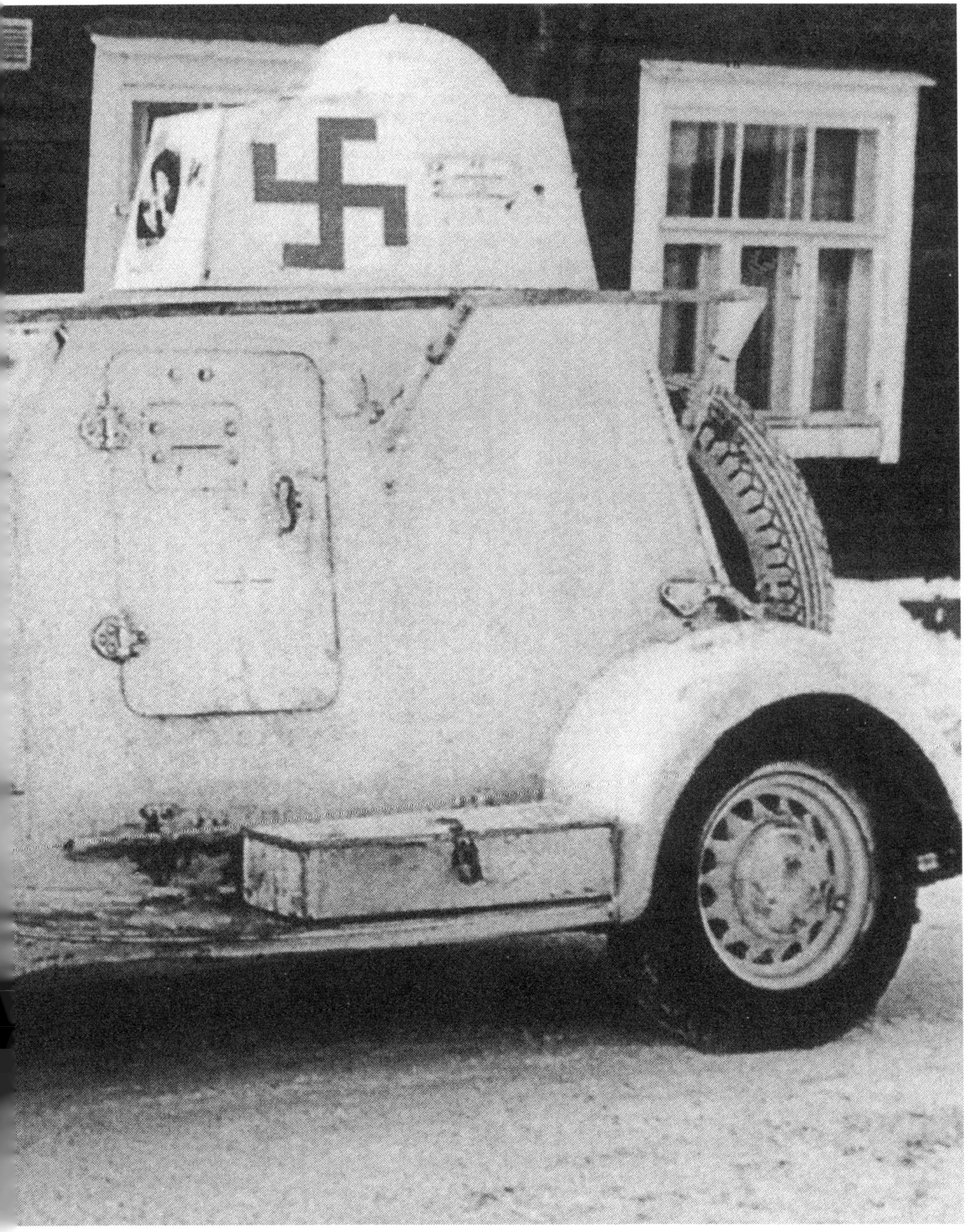

isolated pockets in the Kitelä-Koirinoia-Lemetti-Uomaa sector. Attempts to break out of their encirclement in January were unsuccessful. If necessary, the 168th Division, which was surrounded in a large pocket near Kitela, could be transported over the frozen ice of Ladoga or rescued by air. But for the 18th Rifle Division and the 34th Tank Brigade, which were defending themselves with split garrisons, the situation was very bleak.

In order to relieve the suffering, a sizable unit out of the 8th Army was detached on January 10, 1940, and then reorganized on February 12 as the 15th Army.(the commanding officer was Major General M. Kovalov (later, beginning February 25, Major General V. Kurdjumov took over this command). Included in this army were the encircled units (the 18th and 168th Rifle Divisions and 34th Tank Brigade) in addition to the newly formed 11th, 37th, 60th, and 72nd Rifle Divisions and the 25th Motorized Cavalry Division, along with three airborne brigades. The 15th Army's mission was to re-establish physical contact with the encircled units, occupy the islands of Maksimansaari, Paimionsaari, and Petäjäsaari in Lake Ladoga, and thereafter carry out an offensive advance towards Sordavala.

The offensive began March 6 and by that evening all three islands had been taken and connection had been re-established with the encircled 168th Rifle Division. Towards the end of the war, the army's forces were able to advance some additional kilometres in the direction of Pitkäranta. As to the units out of the 18th Rifle Division and the 34th Tank Brigade – they were all but totally annihilated by the Finns. Only a few isolated groups of soldiers were able to get past the encirclement.

Towards the middle of February, the 8th Army was significantly strengthened by the addition of the 1st Rifle Corps (the 56th, 75th and165th Rifle Divisions, and the 24th Motorized Cavalry Division), the 14th Rifle Corps (the 87th and 128th Rifle Divisions), along with the 139th and 155th Rifle Divisions. The army's mission was to go on the offensive towards Kollaa and crush enemy units at Loimola. On March 12, after intense battle, units of the 8th Army took the Finnish defence line and the Talvela unit pushed south and west.

The tank forces' operations

The terrain in the zones of the 8th and 15th Army consisted solely of woods and swamp with very few roads, and those roads that did exist were for the most part unpaved. In the winter of 1939-40 the snow cover reached a depth of .110-125 cm, and 40-60 cm of ice covered the rivers. The temperature rested at 40 degrees centigrade under zero (Jan 15-18 the temperature bottomed at minus 58!).

TABLE 9. ARMORED VEHICLES IN THE 8TH ARMY'S TANK FORCES ON NOVEMBER 30, 1939.

	T-26	ChT-26, ChT-130	T-37/38	BA-10	FAI
421 otb	11	-	12	-	-
129 orb	-	-	-	-	2
162 orb	-	-	21	6	-
368 otb	16	-	22	-	-
54 orb	-	-	-	5	-
410 otb	15	-	22	-	-
38 orb	-	-	-	10	-
381 otb	17	-	20	-	-
56 orb	-	-	-	7	-
456 otb	12	-	15	-	-
187 orb	-	-	-	9	-
111 otb	54	-	-	-	-
218 chtb	-	31	-	-	-
201 chtb	-	51	-	-	-

(orb = special intelligence battalion , otb = special tank battalion, chtb = special chemical tank battalion)

A T-26, model 1938, captured by the Finns and delegated to the heavy tank platoon of the tank battalion, with the field ID R-43, Hämeenlinna, the fall of 1940.

Here, the Finnish defence was constructed according the lines of battle, the frontal sector and free-standing positions. The main natural defence lines formed along the rivers Tulemajoki, Uksunjoki and Janisjoki. The latter mentioned "natural lines" were the ones most vital for the 8th Army's, and secondarily, even for the 15th Army's advance – as much due to the very demanding terrain conditions – as to the extensive and hard to overcome military installations. All larger communities and crossroads were defence zones, protected by a company or battalion. Not only did Soviet tanks have to struggle against the natural, challenging conditions of the local terrain, but against an effective enemy defence combined of gun fire and man-made, as well as natural, anti-tank obstacles. Against the tanks, the Finns used 37-45 mm anti-tank guns and rifles, minefields, and bottles filled with petrol (there were many of the latter, but they weren't used against tanks in motion, only when disabled), timber barricades, anti-tank trenches, earth-walls, concrete blocks and turret-lines. The 45 mm anti-tank guns in the Finnish arsenal were the captured spoils of having crushed the 75th and the 139th Rifle Divisions. But, overall, the Finnish opposition had a limited number of anti-tank guns. Those they did have were usually placed approximately 800-1000 meters from the road in specially dug out fox-holes and aimed directly in the direction the tanks were expected to appear.

The most effective defence against the tanks were minefields. Getting past them required the use of manually operated detectors and/or T-26's equipped as "mine-sweepers." The first mentioned weren't always effective and, with the snow cover at least a meter deep, the latter passed over the mines without detonating them.

Tanks often wound up in "wolf-pits," a type of anti-tank trap that measured 4 x 6 or 6 x 8 meters in area with a depth of 2-3 meters. Anti-tank trenches with a length of 800-1000 meters were dug as part of comprehensive defence systems that included other obstacles. Escarpments, stretching from 300 to 500 meters, were erected as high as 1.5 meters. Stone baricades were placed on the flanks of other man-made obstacles. These stones were usually 40-50 cm in diameter and 70-100 cm in height, set out in four checkerboard-patterned rows.

Turret-lines were encountered deep within a Finnish defence emplacement. They were rendered harmless by having a tank's main gun blast down one of the trees the line was fastened to.

At the beginning of the war, the 8th Army consisted of: (see table 9)

Assigned to the 8th Army, the 34th Tank Brigade (174 tanks and 25 armored-vehicles) arrived right at the beginning of the war. The brigade was attached to the 18th Rifle Division with the mission of forcing its way behind the frontline of the Finish forces on the Karelian Isthmus. Attempts to use the brigade for this purpose were unsuccessful – after five days of continuous fighting, it hadn't succeeded in making any advance. Even worse, at the end of December 1939, the Finns were able to encircle the 34th Tank Brigade. After having been surrounded, losing all its equipment and a large portion of its troop strength, what remained of the brigade managed to get past the ring in February.

As yet, the only photo found of the commander of the 34th Light Tank Brigade, Brigade Commander Kondratiev. (RIGVA)

The first period of battle revealed that reconnaissance was weakly organized (especially during battle) and that the infantry regarded tanks as the sole and sufficient source of this information. The result was unnecessary losses and delay of the offensive. On December 14, a ChT-26 was transferred from the 201st Tank Battalion to a ski patrol that carried out reconnaissance in the sector bordering Syskyjärvi. When the tank attempted to go around a timber barricade that blocked the road, it drove into a creek and got stuck. The reconnaissance squad came under fire and began to retreat. The tank was left on its own, and no longer accompanied by support, it was destroyed by gun fire and the crew killed.

Lieutenant Naumova's tank (from the 34th Tank Brigade) carried out reconnaissance in the town of Syskyjärvi, which was held by the Finns, and drove over a mine. For a long while, the tank defended itself from the surrounding enemy. Finally, when it burst into flames, the crew abandoned the vehicle and managed, with the help of grenades, to begin working their way back – two days later, the men were able to reunite with their unit.

On December 19, the staff of the 75th Rifle Division sent six T-26's with a 50 man detachment of infantry on an attack against what they believed to be a retreating enemy. The tanks advanced along a road and, unaware,

TABLE 10. INFORMATION REGARDING LOSSES IN THE 8TH ARMY'S TANK FORCES FROM NOVEMBER 30, 1939 UNTIL MARCH 13, 1940 (EXCL. THE 18TH AND 168TH RIFLE DIVISION, THE 201ST CHEMICAL TANK BATTALION AND THE 34TH LIGHT TANK BRIGADE).

Type of armored vehicle	Took part in battle	Losses		Total Losses
		Due to artillery fire	mines	
T-26	247	56	9	65
ChT-26, 130	47	21	5	26
T-37/ T-38	54	17	5	22
BA-10	39	7	3	10
BA-20	23	3	-	3

were allowed to venture deep into a Finnish position where they were fired upon and destroyed. Reconnaissance methods were considerably improved as time went on.

The attacks undertaken during the first period of combat operations were consistently badly organized. No echelon formations were employed – the enemy wasn't destroyed but rather driven away and the tanks were utilized in an uninformed and inexperienced way. For example, the headquarter section of the 56th Rifle Division accepted delivery of ChT-26 type tanks, which markedly differed from the 52 T-26 tanks that were in its division at the time. The result was that these tanks were put out of action the first time they encountered fire from anti-tank weapons.

Again, during this first period, tanks appeared to prefer moving along the roads but, as time went on and more experience gained, they preferred, for the most part, to make their way off-road. And while there was a marked slowdown in the tempo of travel, the same can be said about the tempo of losses, and attacks became decidedly more successful. Methods of overcoming anti-tank obstacles also changed. And while tank crews during the first period had to rely solely on themselves to go through minefields and set bridges over trenches, towards the end of the war, infantry and engineer units lent their assistance. Reconnaissance missions perceptibly improved and seldom were tanks seen falling into camouflaged pits or trenches.

In the very beginning of the war, co-operation among tank, infantry, and artillery units was well organized, especially in the lower ranks, as between tank platoons and rifle companies. But after the first few days of combat, where the resistance had been weak, criteria necessary to co-operation were gradually neglected – operations were simplified and sometimes co-ordination between units was completely lacking.

For example, on December 18, the commander of the 208th Rifle Regiment gave orders to the commanding officer of the 76th Tank Battalion to provide support for the regiment's attack against Syskyjävi. The tank company's commander led an attack against Syskyjävi without having co-ordinated his actions with anyone. The Finns were driven out, but the infantry didn't follow with the tanks. As a result, the Finns mounted a counter-

A type ChT-130 tank on a courtyard at the Vorosjilov Factory no. 174. (ASKM)

Soviet tank personnel checking out a Finnish tank helmet found in a Vickers in the vicinity of Honkaniemi, Feb. 1940. (ASKM)

A column of BA-10 armored cars from the 29th Light Tank Brigade on a street in Viborg, March 13, 1940. (ASKM)

A ChT-134 tank being tested in Kubinka, the summer of 1940. The fl ame-thrower on the body work's upper plate is easily seen. The tank arrived at the Karelian Isthmus where it took part in battles. In order to bring down its weight before being tested, the extra armoured plating was removed which simultaneously makes the turret easier to see. (ASKM)

The radio mechanized "group" the "Exploder" being tested on the Karelian Isthmus, Mar. 1940. The control tank is shown on the photo immediately above – the tank being radio controlled is shown on the topmost photo. (N. Gavrilkin)

attack and succeeded in driving the tanks from the town, and the contended point, Syskyjävi, continued to be held by the enemy.

On December 14, the Finns in the Kollanjärvi district launched an attack against the 37th Rifle Regiment, which hastily retreated, leaving the regiment's artillery and anti-tank gun units without protection. On the basis of rushed and unclear orders given by the regiment's commander, a platoon from the 111th Tank Battalion went to the artillery's assistance. The platoon leader, Lieutenant Podlutskij, cast his unit into battle without a clear idea of the objective, without knowledge of the terrain, and without having co-ordinated his input with the infantry. After having helped the artillery, the platoon, due to a lack of familiarity with the area, wound up in an anti-tank trench and couldn't get out. They were all killed by anti-tank weapons.

But, by taking care to well-organize all the different units involved in a military operation, the probability of a mission's success greatly increases: On December 9, 1939, a battalion out of the 184th Rifle Regiment became surrounded. A platoon from the 111th Tank Battalion was singled out to lead a breakthrough attempt. The platoon leader, Lieutenant Tjernov, planned his mission in comprehensive detail and organized a co-operative effort, not only within his platoon, but with the infantry and the gun support of tanks, as well. Executing the attack in two echelons, the platoon broke through the enemy's ring – and without losses – led the battalion out, covered its retreat, and secured the formation of a new line. In January, a unit with the 8th Army's tank forces organized an orientation lecture for newly arrived tank units, emphasizing the special conditions tank forces faced in carrying out their operations in the Finnish terrain with

Same tank as shown on page 110, though from a somewhat different angle, middle south Lemetti, Feb. 1940. (Tank Museum)

Trophy captured by the Red Army being shown at the "Crushing of the White-Finns" exhibition: a Vickers BT, Leningrad, Mar. 1940. (ASKM)

its lakes, forests and swamps – and the tactics of tank units in combat. Before every battle, mutual inter-unit training was organized with supporting infantry and artillery. Tank crews received instruction about the local terrain conditions and training in driving tanks off-road and methods to overcome anti-tank obstacles. All this preparation gave rise to good results in the battles that took place in March 1940.

The battles that occurred under encirclement, such as those conducted in January-February by units of the 34th Tank Brigade, the 201st Special Chemical Battalion and the 381st Special Tank Battalion with the 18th Rifle Division, were not characteristic, since the tanks took no active measures to break through the encirclement. In addition, it should be noted that they had set up a narrow defence zone along the road in Södra Lemetti – approximately two kilometres long, with a width that varied between 120-600 meters – but a lack of fuel prevented them from making maneuvers and the tanks were therefore used only as fixed firing installations.

In defensive situations, the tanks were mainly used to secure connections and flanks, as well as to protect roads and command emplacements. In many of these situations there was no protective support from the infantry and this deficiency was exploited by the Finns who during the night would bring up anti-tank guns on sleds and blast the tanks out of commission. It was precisely in this way that two vehicles in the 111th Tank Battalion were set afire. The tanks played a positive roll with regard to throwing back enemy attacks. Towing of vehicles disabled in combat was carried out by army units and the 19th Tractor Towing Company. This unit had at its disposal 34 STZ-3 tractors that were requisitioned from civilian households, and over the course of battle they towed away 119 T-26's, 16 T-37's, 9 BA's, 120 T-20's and 1,622 cars and trucks.

The army's tank forces were poorly equipped in terms of repair resources. At the beginning of hostilities, only 54 percent of the stipulated total of mobile repair "type A" facilities existed – as to "type B" facilities, only 16 percent of the stipulated total existed.. Moreover, access to tools and equipment at many repair facilities was woefully insufficient. A work brigade sent from Factory no.174 undertook a great number of repairs and beginning January 1, 1940, it carried out 362 routine and 153 middle level tank repairs and 110 armored car repairs. Tank units were continuously compensated for losses during the entire course of the war: The 8th Army received ten T-26's, five BT-7's, 69 ChT-!33's and 50 BA-20's. The 15th Army received 129 T-26 tanks. Among these, were 15 reinforced T-26's that arrived just as the war ended.

The 34th light tank brigade

The commanding officer was Brigade Commander S. Kondratiev and the commissioner was Regimental Commissioner Gapanjuk. The brigade was formed under the auspices of the "large education maneuver" on the basis of being a reserve unit of the 2nd Armored Regiment from the city of Naro-Frominsk. By September 21 the brigade had acquired its final pre-war structure consisting of the 76th, 82nd, 83rd and 86th Tank Battalions, the 224th Reconnaissance Battalion, the 1st Motorized Rifle Battalion, the 274th Repair and Maintenance Battalion and the 322nd Motor Vehicle Transportation Battalion, along with the 23rd Combat-Supply Company, the 62nd Engineer Company, the 84th Liaison Company and the 324th Medicine and Medical Care Company – all told, there were 237 tanks (in the main, BT-5's from various units in the Moscow Military District), 25 armored vehicles, 13 tractors, 41 mobile "type A" repair facilities and 21 of "type B," 73 armored cars and 317 cars and trucks. The military equipment was in satisfactory shape but the brigade commander reported that, "The brigade, due to demobilization, is not sufficiently supplied with armored car and tank accessories: Many tanks lack tarpaulins, and the brigade is not provided with frost-protection salve, nor is it entirely provided with regard to repair crews, armored cars and vehicles for medical purposes and staff requirements. The tractors, which have been collected from civilian households, require fundamental repairs and are therefore to be returned." The personnel were well trained but were completely inexperienced about what must be done under the conditions that prevailed in Finland. The commander of the brigade, Brigade Commander Kontratiev, had already gained combat experience – under the Spanish Civil War he'd had charge of the 1st International Tank Brigade and been decorated with the Order of Lenin. In the beginning of October 1939, the brigade was sent to the Lithuanian border and in the beginning of December it was placed in the 8th Army. The 86th Armored Battalion was detached from the brigade and transferred to the Murmansk area.

On December 13, the brigade was attached to the 56th Rifle Corps and assigned the mission of launching an attack against Sordavala, as a first step in forcing its way behind the line of Finnish forces on the Karelian Isthmus. During the period December 14-17, extended tank battles took place around Syskyjärvi and Uomaa, but success was not achieved in either of these locations. The local natural conditions (forests, swamps and blocks of stone) did not lend themselves to the use of massive tank formations and all battles were confined to maneuvers on narrow roads.

In addition, the 56th Corps' leadership, in effect, split the brigade when tanks were deployed for purposes that did not accord with its combat role or mission, such as patrolling roads behind the front, or protecting the airfield or staff headquarters.

As a follow of this, the Finns cut off the brigade from units of the 56th Corps in the course of carrying out a counter-attack on Jan 1-2, 1940. A comprehensive defence was then organized by the 34th brigade's staff in Södra Lemetti, wherein a combined rifle battalion was created consisting of engineer troops, communications personnel and subordinates under the brigade's command from the home-front – in all, 450 men were included in this defence. Radio contact with the brigade's other units – encircled in Norra Lemetti and Mitro – was established by Brigade Commander Kondratiev. Two companies with the 179th Motorized Rifle Battalion attempted to break through to Lemetti, but this try was unsuccessful. On January 4, the Finns cut off the road between Södra and Norra Lemetti, resulting in the brigade then being split up into three sections. In Södra Lemetti, the brigade's staff, along with subdivisions – namely, the 83rd Tank Battalion (less a company) and the 224th Reconnaissance Battalion – enlisted from among the units stationed behind the front, continued to defend themselves: In Norra Lemetti, the 76th Tank Battalion, likewise defended itself. And lastly, in Mitro, one company out of the 179th Motorized Rifle Battalion, and one company out of the 83rd Tank Battalion, along with a reconnaissance platoon from the infantry, also sought to defend themselves. Contact between the three groups had been severed. Over the period January 5-14 the Finns continued their attacks against the three encircled units, whose situation worsened from one day to the next. The commander of the 76th Tank Battalion, Captain S. Rjazanov, sent several massages to the brigade commander over the radio: "Come to the rescue – I have heavy losses!" The answer heard: "Hold out with your own strength – No help is coming." Rjazanov then assembled the battalion's officers in order to organize and plan the mission of breaking out of the encirclement. But the authorized representative of the Special Division of the NKVD (the alpha and omega of the Interior Ministry), who happened to be with this battalion group, accused the battalion commander of being cowardly and forbid a breakout from the encirclement. Rjazanov then responded, "I am the commander of this battalion and you will carry out my orders!" At which point, the NKVD man shot and killed the battalion commander. The consequences of this incident soon became apparent: On February 4, there remained only 19 men of the 76th battalion and these men were able to make their way to the brigade staff in Södra Lemetti.

In January, the brigade could still have escaped the encirclement if its vehicles were left behind. At the end of that month, Kondratiev took up the question of breaking out of the encirclement with the commands of the 56th Corps and the 8th Army. In the brigade, sleds and skis were made ready to take everything away with them – There was still fuel left (albeit very little) and there were provisions and ammunition. But the commander of the 8th Army, G. Sjtern, forbid a breakout and sent a radio message: "Hold on, help's coming!" As a result, the brigade spent yet another month in encirclement without any sort of outside support. Many were stricken with night-blindness due to exhaustion, which enabled the Finns to approach the infantry trenches at night and bomb them with grenades. The enemy was especially active through February 18-21. During this period, elements from the brigade entrenched in Mitro united with units out of the 168th Rifle Division and, together, they continued to battle from within the encirclement until the end of the war. During the night of February 8, the units in Södra Lemetti, divided into three groups, began to break out of their encirclement. Of the 850 men who had found themselves surrounded, only 171 reached the safety of their own lines. At the time of the breakout, the following high-ranking personnel shot themselves: the commander of the brigade, Brigade Commander Kondratiev; the brigade's commissioner, Regimental Commissioner Gapanjuk; the head of the political section, Regimental Commissioner Tepluchin; and lastly, the head of the special division, Doronkin. Apparently, all these leaders understood that they would have executed by a firing squad in any event, accused and convicted of traitorous and cowardly conduct

The parties responsible for the brigade having been crushed were, first off, the commands of the 8th Army, the 56th Rifle Corps and the 34th Tank Brigade who lacked necessary knowledge about the enemy. The dearth of co-ordinated combat operations between the 168th and 18th Rifle Divisions and the 34th Tank Brigade, and the tactical failure of not providing flank protection during the offensive which allowed Finns to intercept communications and easily slip behind the advancing units. In addition, orders aimed at bringing about an organized retreat were not given in time – and later – orders were not given in time to breakout of the encirclement while it was still possible to do so (in January). When all is said and done, a breakout was forbidden and the brigade was thereby consigned to its fate.

The result was needlessly tragic: Of the 3,787 men under arms on December 4, 902 were killed, 414 wounded, 94 became sick of suffered from freezing, 291 simply disappeared – in all, 1,701 men (almost 50 percent!) – 27 high-ranking personnel were killed, included in this number were all the battalion commanders.

In a report submitted on March 23 to the commander-and-chief of the Armored Vehicle Command, Corps Commander D. Pavlov, concerning equipment losses from the location of the 34th Tank Brigade's downfall, appears the following: "The brigade's tanks located in Norra Lemetti – 25, Södra Lemetti – 33, Uomos – 9, Mitro – 20, along the Lavojärvi-Uomos road – 19, the Konpinaja train stop – 2, along the road between Norra and Södra Lemetti – 9. Total 117. The brigade has 27 tanks in operation, with the 8th Army's staff there are 3, and with SPAM 8. Total 48. 11 vehicles have not been located, a search is underway. All tanks have been set out of combat shape by the enemy: weapons, instruments, radios and ammunition have been removed and taken away. The turrets and the underside of the turrets of all tanks have been cut off with welding torches and taken away."

This is the location of the main breakthrough in the Mannerheim Line – near height 65.5. In this photo, taken after the fighting, can be seen two disabled type T-28 tanks from the 20th Heavy Tank Brigade Feb. 1940. (CAFM)

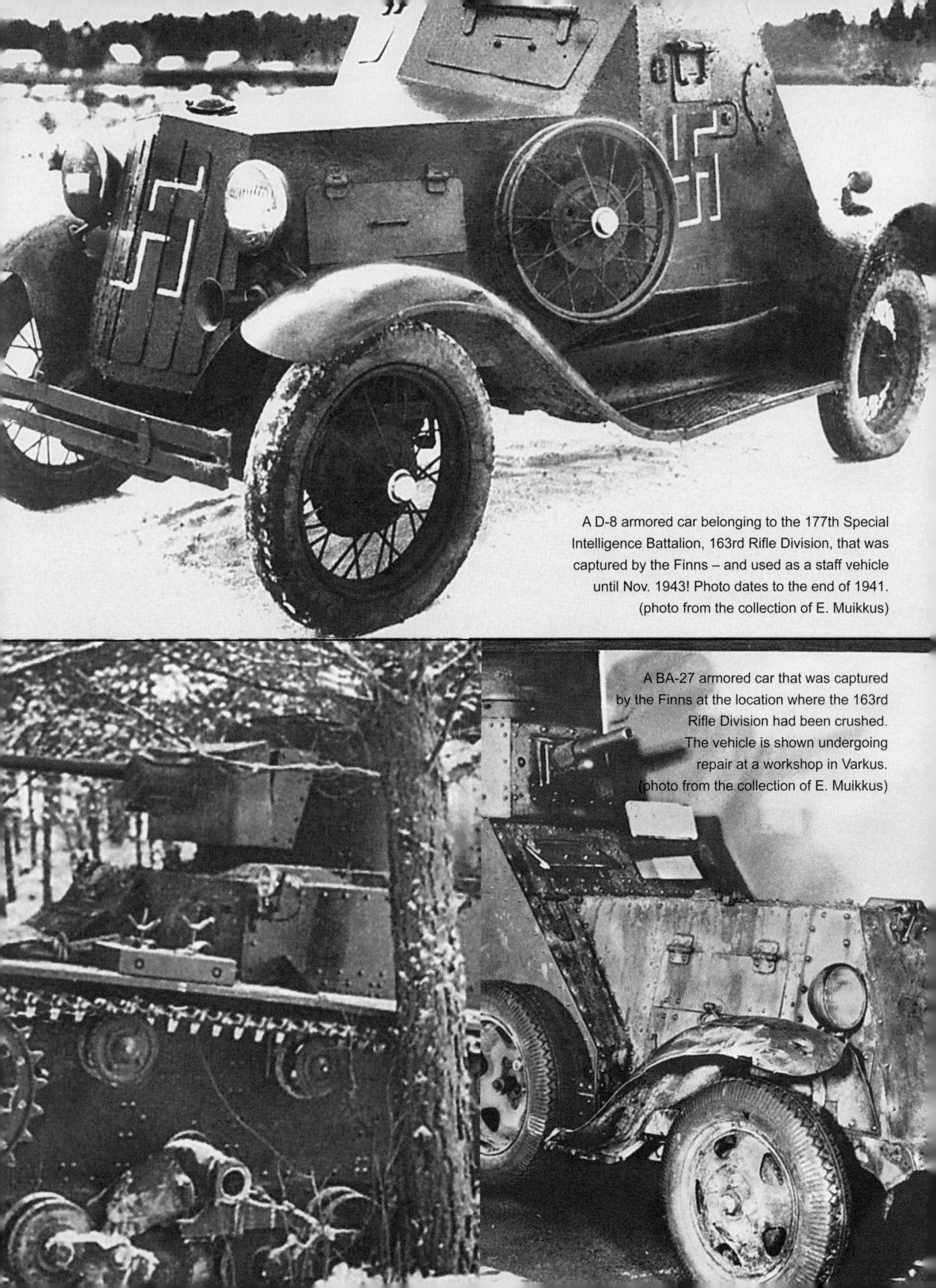

A D-8 armored car belonging to the 177th Special Intelligence Battalion, 163rd Rifle Division, that was captured by the Finns – and used as a staff vehicle until Nov. 1943! Photo dates to the end of 1941.
(photo from the collection of E. Muikkus)

A BA-27 armored car that was captured by the Finns at the location where the 163rd Rifle Division had been crushed. The vehicle is shown undergoing repair at a workshop in Varkus.
(photo from the collection of E. Muikkus)

3:4 Battles in the 9th army sector

The course of battle in general

In the beginning of the war, the 9th Army, commanded by Corps Commander M. Duchanov (on December 22, this position was assumed by Corps Commander V.Tjujkov), consisted of the Special Rifle Corps and the 47th Rifle Corps (the 44th, 54th, 122nd, and the 163rd Rifle Divisions. The army's mission was to advance to Oulu and in this way divide Finland in two sections.

The prevailing conditions under which these battles were fought were even more severe than those in the 8th Army sector. The weather was forbidding, dwellings were seldom encountered, the network of roadways was extremely sparse and the roads themselves were narrow. A joined front was therefore neither practical nor possible and there were tens of kilometers between the advancing divisions.

The 54th Division moved forward in the direction of Reboly-Kuhmo and after only a week of battle it had pushed its way 50 kilometers into Finland. The Vuokko Brigade, which had been hastily formed by the Finnish command, halted this early offensive after intense battle, and in January, it succeeded in surrounding units from the 54th Division in the Rasti district. The division's commander, Brigade Commander Gusevkij, was able to organize an overall defence and, from January 29 to March 13, the division carried on battles from within the area of its encirclement with split garrisons.

By December 16, the 122nd Rifle Division, advancing in the direction of Kandalksja-Salla had covered 200 kilometers, after having fought back the opposing Finnish forces. On December 18, Finnish units from Major General K. Wallinius' "Lapland force" (the 8th Infantry Battalion) launched a counter-attack against the 122nd Rifle Division, which was forced to change over to defence, after having been driven back 20 kilometers. From then on, the front remained stable in this area until the end of the war.

The 163rd Rifle Division went on the offensive in Uchta advancing in the direction of Suomussalmi. From December 11 to Dec.28, the Finnish 9th Infantry Battalion under Colonel H. Siilasvuo pursued a counter-attack forcing the 163rd Division back: Its units retreated in disorder along Lake Kiantajärvi and took up defensive positions in the Juntusranta district. On January 2, the 44th Rifle Division, which had been sent to rescue the 163rd Rifle Division, also became encircled. It had been transferred to the Karelian Isthmus from the Ukraine shortly before the war started, and its personnel had no experience of conducting combat operations under the local conditions of deep snow, and terrain entirely made up of forests, swamps and lakes. The commander of the 44th Rifle Division, Brigade Commander Vinograndov, who had been promoted from battalion commander to division commander within the space of a year, couldn't organize a breakout from the encirclement in an "appropriate" operation and, by January 7, the division had been almost totally decimated. The 44th Rifle Division's commander, its commissioner and its chief-of-staff were executed before a troop formation for "treachery and cowardice."

At the end of January, an operation unit was created in the Rebol sector, under the command of Division Commander Niikitov, with the objective of freeing the 54th Rifle Division. On February 2, this unit began an offensive, but due to the bitter cold and a raging snowstorm it couldn't carry out its mission.

Beginning February 22, the 9th Army Corps started to ready itself for the coming offensive, planned for March 15-17. Pre-offensive battles began March 7 with an attack launched by the 163rd Rifle Division, but the plan was never set in motion due to a cease fire.

The tank force's operations

At the war's outset, the 9th Army's tank forces consisted of the 177th Special Reconnaissance Battalion with 122nd Rifle Division (17 T-37's and two armored cars), and a special reconnaissance battalion with the 163rd Rifle Division (12 T-37's, two T-38's and two BA-27's).

In the beginning, the tanks were used for reconnaissance, combat protection and liaison missions. Thereafter – which is to say, as soon as the 163rd Division began advancing towards Peranka-Suomussalmi – this modest number of tanks was divided among the rifle divisions. After 15 days of battle, nearly all the tanks had been disabled by mine explosions..

Over the period December 5 to Dec. 27, the 9th Army was augmented by the addition of the 100th, the 79th, the 365th, the 302nd and the 97th Special Tank Battalions, along with the 44th Rifle Division, which also included the 312th Tank Battalion and the 4th Reconnaissance Battalion, each with 47 T-26's. Among these, could be found tanks equipped with guns and machines guns dating from 1931, including Hotchkiss 37 mm guns, for which the army would have no grenades in its munitions throughout the war. The 302nd Battalion had only seven double-turreted T-26 tanks (six with machine guns, and one with both a machine gun and a heavy gun) and this battalion didn't participate in battle.

The equipment in all battalions was extensively worn – and 50 percent of the vehicles only had engine resources (fuel, oil, antifreeze, etc.) for 50-75 hours running at the

Abandoned russian tanks model BT-5, in the Lemetti cauldron (motti), February 1940-

Captured Soviet ChT-26 tank being repaired at a workshop in Varkus, the spring of 1940. A hole caused by an anti-tank grenade is visible on the front section of the turret. The ChT tanks that were captured by the Finns were only used for training, after first removing the flame thrower. (photo from the collection of E. Muikkus)

most. As soon as the battalions arrived they were assigned to the rifle divisions, and they participated in battles together with the respective divisions they had been assigned to. It should also be noted that, for the most part, the tanks had travelled the 180-270 kilometers distance from the unloading platform under their own steam. This led to each battalion having to leave off 7-10 vehicles for total restoration on arrival and the time required for this work took 5-15 days.

The battalions were poorly supplied with spare parts and lacked necessary repair resources (materials, tools and equipment). The units had been hastily formed and consequently the soldiers barely knew each other and hadn't been instructed in shooting, nor had the corps of drivers been trained in how to carry out their job under harsh winter conditions and hilly terrain.

Satisfactory co-operation among tanks, infantry, and artillery was never realized, nor was a communications system for co-ordinating activities established, and reconnaissance was badly carried out. Splitting up battalions into sub-units smaller than a company, and especially with respect to certain vehicles (which took place during the first period of fighting), often had negative consequences. The harsh terrain conditions – mountains, forests, snow (up to 120 cm) and bitter cold (as low as minus 50 centigrade) – significantly hindered the use of tanks. Nevertheless, attacks – if they were well-thought out and co-ordination with infantry and artillery established – were successful. On December 8, a tank company from the 100th battalion, in co-operation with an accompanying infantry unit, thwarted an enemy ambush on the outskirts of Kuokojärvi that had attacked their flank from the rear. This turned out to be a prelude the city's fall, which occurred the following night of December 9.

On December 11, the 100th Tank Battalion advanced, by means of a bold maneuver, towards Märkäjärvi and attacked retreating Finnish units and transportation vehicles, capturing 8 machine guns, 25,000 rounds of ammunition, and many grenades and mines. The enemy fled in panic, with no time to blow up a bridge or reorganize the units. As a result, Märkäjärvi fell. On December 6-7, a tank platoon from the 97th battalion, in close co-operation with artillery, blasted firing installations and

Anti-tank obstacles at the Kollaa front.

Abandoned russian BT-7 tanks on the Raate road in January 1940.

Last line of defense: Finnish soldiers fighting the Read army onslaught from very improvised positions.

A abandoned BA-6 armored car that belonged to 4th Independent Recce Battalion from the 44th Rifle Division in the 9th Army. It fought at Raate in January 1940.

The Raate road jammed with abandoned russian trucks. January 1940.

As far as one can see, only abandoned T-20 Komsomolets tracked tractors outside Suomussalmi in Januaru 1940. As much as possible the Finnish army took over all the russian equipment.

A long line of barbed wire obstacles at the Kollaa front.

blinds on the isthmus between the lakes Alasjärvi and Saunajärvi, and thereby opened the way for the 337th Rifle Regiment to occupy the isthmus.

Throughout the entire operation it was the 100th Tank Battalion who contributed the most successful input. Assigned independent objectives, it boldly left the road and maneuvered the tanks over the natural terrain. However, this positive experience did not generate the dissemination it warranted, and many commanders, including even tank drivers, maintained right through the end of the war that tanks, given the prevailing terrain conditions, could not be deployed other than on the available roads. Reconnaissance via tanks, as a rule, did produce hoped for results because this task was performed by solitary tanks without the input or co-operation of the infantry and this, in turn, led to the loss of tanks. In the Juntusranta district, for example, a lone tank out of the 79th Tank Battalion rolling ahead of the infantry on point, touched off a mine and exploded. An infantry unit saw this happen but didn't venture to help and as a result the tank crew was killed.

Above all else, poor co-operation with other combat entities, such as infantry and artillery, and unsatisfactory reconnaissance were the usual causes of misguided operations with tragic consequences. Such a tragedy befell a platoon out of the 100th Tank Battalion: On December 14, 1939, the platoon launched an attack against Finnish positions in the Kursu district, without having first sought pre-assault artillery bombardment on the enemy. Only a short while thereafter, the only anti-tank gun the Finns possessed sighted and hit five tanks. As a result, nine men died – among them, the battalion's chief-of-staff.

In the district of Kornisalmi, five tank platoons from the 97th Tank Battalion, without reconnaissance or pre-assault artillery fire, attacked a forward sector of the enemy's defence. As a result, three vehicles were exploded by mines and it wasn't until two days of battle had passed before the crews were able to reunite with their unit. During an operation with the 44th Rifle Division, a tank out of the 312th Tank Battalion went on ahead and became cut off from the infantry by the Finns employing a wooden barricade. As a result, the tank crew, under the command of Lieutenant Ivantjuk, fought from within

an encirclement for five days before it was finally freed towards the end of the fifth day by other Soviet forces. From the beginning of January until the war's end, Soviet forces maintained a defensive posture, not engaging in any aggressive attacks in the Kandalksja-and-Uchta Sector. The tanks were used in limited numbers to protect command points and roads. The latter proved to be ineffective since the Finns generally cut off the roads at night.

In the battles carried out by the 163rd Rifle Division to free the 54th Rifle Division from encirclement, tanks were used to support the infantry from March 8 until the end of the war.

During the entire war, the tank forces of the 9th Army suffered a lack of spare parts and repair and towing resources. There were only three roads that lead out from the supply base, which meant that these were the only roads on which necessities could be delivered – and of course – they were constantly attacked by the enemy. Repair equipment for the army was therefore confined to one repair train which sat parked at the Kem railway station and, for all practical purposes, the battalion's mobile repair facilities lacked both tools and materials. And for all practical purposes, the tank forces had, on the whole, no towing resources of their own. The Army's towing company was augmented with STZ-5 type tractors, but due to the low horsepower of their engines they couldn't be used to pull tanks. Attempts to use "Komsomolets" tow-vehicles were likewise unsuccessful because they lacked sufficient traction.

Again, in practical terms, no strengthening of forces in connection with receiving new equipment took place – During the war, the army took delivery of only ten BA-10's. In order to protect transportation columns, the 54th armored car battalion constructed an armored truck, the GAZ-AA, in March 1940. Its driver's cab and engine were protected with 3.7 mm steel plate and armed with a "Maxim" type machine gun or a DP, mounted beside the driver. This improvised armored truck earned a good reputation as an escort vehicle for transportation columns.

During the entire course of the war, human casualties with 9th Army's tank forces mounted to 119 killed, 154 wounded, 61 frozen to death, and 92 missing in action.

Armoured tractors model T-20 Komsomolets with 45-mm AT-guns in tow, on their way towards the front. Karelian Isthmus, close to Vaskelovo on the 2nd of December 1939.

The commander of the 10th Tank Corps, P. Versjinin (in this photo from 1945, he carries the rank of Lieutenant General). (RIGVA)

The commander of the 1st Light Tank Brigade, V. Ivanov (in this photo from 1945 he carries the rank of Major General). (RIGVA)

A 76 mm Kurtjevski gun (mounted on a truck, model GAZ-TK), the War Museum in Helsinki. (ASKM)

TABLE 11. INFORMATION REGARDING LOSSES IN THE 9TH ARMY'S TANK PORCES FROM NOVEMBER 30, 1939 UNTIL MARS 13, 1940.

Type of armored vehicle	Losses				
	Due to Artillery fire	mines	fire	Sunk in water	Left in enemy territory
T-26	5	8	2	1	14
T-37/ T-38	7	18	-	2	16
T-20 "Komsomolets"	2	11	1	-	7
BA-27	-	-	-	-	2
BA-20	-	-	2	-	1
BA-6	2	3	-	-	2
BA-3	-	-	-	-	2
D-8	-	-	-	-	3
SPK	-	-	-	-	2

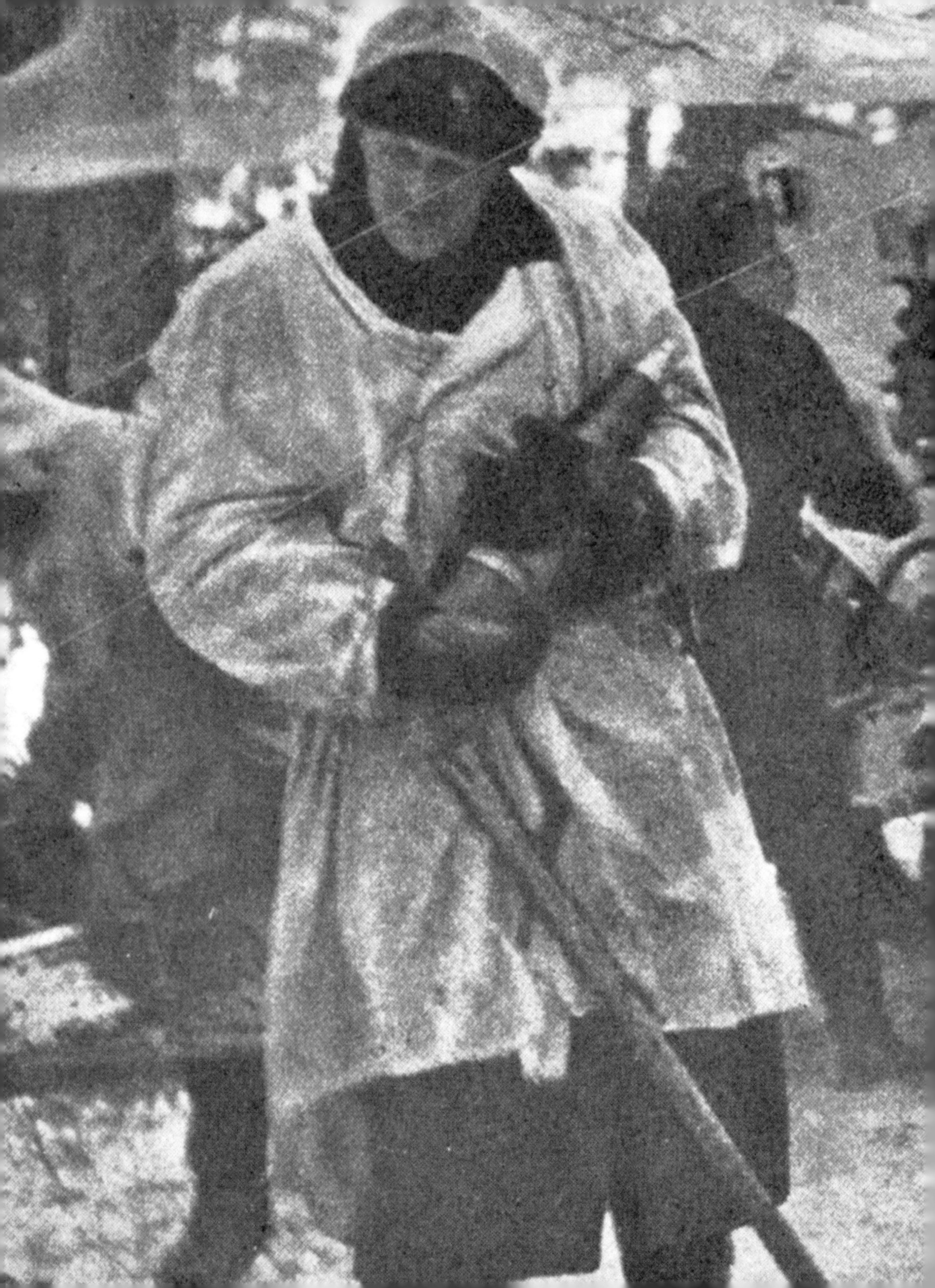

The backbone of the Finnish defenses, the artillery. Often it was only thanks to the Finnish artillery and it´s deadly fi re, that Russian tank attacks could be stopped.

This rather unsharp photo shows two T-26 attacking Finnish positions at Kollaa. The tank on the right has just been hit by anti-tank fire, while the one on the left still are advancing.

Deserted Russian equipment after the destruction of the Motti at Lemetti.

Deserted BT-7 tanks in the Motti at Lemetti.

The Finnish forces also operated armored trains. They used them with telling effect in Karelia.

Russian artillery pieces in the Motti of Lemetti.

BT-7 tanks (with cylindrical turrets and rod shaped antennas) and T-28's from the 20th Tank Brigade just outside Viborg, Northwest Front, Mar. 1940. All tanks are repainted white. (ASKM)

3:5 The fighting in the Murmansk sector

The course of fighting in general

At the beginning of the war, the 14th Army (led by Corps Commander V. Frolov), consisting of the 52nd and the 104th Rifle Divisions, was assigned to occupy the Petsamo district and hinder the transport of troops and equipment through the Norwegian port of Kirkenes. Without encountering any serious problem, units of these divisions occupied the peninsulas of Rybatiij and Srednij, as well as the Petsamo ports of Liinahamari and Luostari: Over eight days of battle, they had advanced 150 kilometers. The Finnish force from the "Lapplandia" section (led by Major General K. Wallenius), with a combat strength of only three battalions, was naturally not able to halt the advance of two Red Army divisions. By December 18, the Soviet forces had reached Höyhenjärvi where they broke off their offensive. Keeping these forces supplied was made difficult by the long distances involved, and the natural surroundings of an artic location and polar nights hindered active fighting. Weather conditions were incredibly severe: Temperatures dipped under minus 50 degrees centigrade and brutal snowstorms raged through the area. Despite this, the activities of the Finnish and Soviet ski patrols were fairly intensive. On February 24, for example, the Finns surrounded a ski patrol (total 153 men) out of the 52nd Division and it required the strength of an entire battalion to free them.

On March 6, the Soviet forces resumed their offensive. After Nautsi was taken, the Finns withdrew south and the Red Army forces changed over to a defensive posture. The front in this area remained stable for the remainder of the war.

The activities of the armored units

The natural conditions north of the polar circle were very unfavorable to tank force operations. Deeply pocked broken ground covered with stone blocks, mountains and hills, steep cliffs and deep snow – all this diminished the usefulness of tanks.

The Finnish forces employed a "fight on the run" defensive method. As they withdrew south, they destroyed roads and constructed obstacles of felled trees, along with laying mines and explosive charges. In the Pitko-Järvi district, anti-tank obstacles and walls made of timber were erected, walls of ice as high as 1.5 meters were also constructed and anti-tank trenches were dug up to a meter deep. On lakes, the Finns blew up the ice in front of their foremost positions, creating wide holes in the ice. The engineers' installations were covered by anti-tank gun fire, but these attacks were usually of short duration because the Finns abstained from all out battles. The army's tank force was used to strengthen the infantry units, to protect the command staff and communications, for patrolling, and for escorting transport columns and liaison vehicles.

At the beginning of the war, the 14th Army had three tank battalions and two reconnaissance battalions.

The 83rd Special Tank Battalion (53 BT-5's), which had come from the 34th Tank Brigade, had inappropriate military equipment, and personnel who were unprepared for carrying out combat operations under the winter conditions that prevailed in the far north. The "mud-feet" on the BT-5 tanks weren't dubbed and the tanks, struggling mightily to get over steep rises and hills covered with a sheet of ice – often slid off the road.

The 411th Special Tank Battalion (15 T-26's and 15 T-38's) came to Murmansk from the 4th Army in the White Russian Military District. The vehicles were badly worn but the crews were well-trained and the drivers were fairly well experienced. During the repair process, from November 23 to December 6, all the tanks were put into shape and six T-26 engines were replaced. .

The 349th Special Tank Battalion's (12 T-26's and 15 T-37/38's) complement of vehicles had been strengthened at the beginning of the war by additions from the training regiment at Leningrad's Armored Vehicle Technical College. Over a period extending from shortly before the war to its end, all the tanks had required middle-level repairs in Murmansk and Petsamo. As much as 70 percent of the tank crew personnel were drawn from the reserves and were poorly trained.

The 35th Special Reconnaissance Battalion (one FAI and six T-27's), all other problems aside, had no combat vehicles to begin with – but before the war broke out, this oversight was addressed with vehicles obtained from various infantry units.

The 65th Special Reconnaissance Battalion (ten BA-3's/10's) was strengthened by its cadre of drivers who had received a good deal of practical training by haven driven tanks in the invasion of White Russia (Belarus).

In addition, 19 small T-27 tanks and 35 "Komsomolets" T-20 tow-vehicles were included in the infantry units' complement.

The fighting developed along a very thin front line, making it possible to deploy from two to five tanks directly on the battlefield. In the main, two to three T-26's were deployed in co-operation with a rifle company or battalion.

Tanks from the 411th Tank Battalion attached to the 59th Rifle Division appear to have been the most active.

An assault unit prepares to attack a concrete bunker (DOT). In the foreground, engineers are clad in white gowns for camouflage. In the background, a BT-7 type tank (with a conical turret) out of the 13th Light Tank Brigade. The vehicle is winter camouflaged and a red star adorns its corner, this picture was taken in the area of Hottinen, Jan, 1 1940. (ASKM)

A column of T-26 tanks out of the 11th Special Tank Battalion on the move, 8th Army Zone, Dec. 1939. The tank in the middle is equipped with a spotlight for night combat. (ASKM)

Finnish Bofors 37 mm anti-tank gun captured by the Red Army, Karelian Isthmus, Feb. 1940, (ASKM)

Finnish Bofors 37 mm anti-tank gun captured by the Red Army, Karelian Isthmus, Feb. 1940, (ASKM)

When crossing the Selmajärvi River, the ice broke and two T-26's sunk to the bottom. On December 12, some 95 kilometers from the border, the tanks came up against a timber barricade and a mined road, defended by a company of Finns. When the Finns saw they couldn't hold out against the tanks attacks, they retreated. The 411th Battalion pursued them for 15 kilometers.

From December 26 to February 25, the battalion operated from a defensive position. During this time, the tanks worked alongside the infantry on reconnaissance patrols and on six occasions a tank exploded due to mines. To counter this problem, the battalion, using its own resources and personnel, constructed a "mine trawler" that could be mounted to the front of the tank.

On February 25, a tank platoon under the command of Lieutenant Ivanov (five T-26's), together with infantry from the 205th Rifle Regiment, attempted a break through to extricate an encircled ski patrol. As a result, one tank exploded due to a mine and three were hit by anti-tank gun fire. The ski patrol remained encircled until February 28, when four T-26 tanks accompanied by an infantry battalion out of the 205th Rifle Regiment finally succeeded in freeing them.

The 86th Tank Battalion was concentrated in the Petsamo area until December 3. On December 14, the battalion set out towards the Solomijärvi district in order to provide support to the 52nd Rifle Division's advance. The march-route was very demanding and the track belts on the BT-5's couldn't get a good grip on the ground surface: Only five tanks were able to struggle on for two weeks and reach Solomijärvi under their own power. The rest, after having exhausted their fuel, were towed by tractors. On January 27, the entire battalion once again was concentrated in the Petsamo district, where they were assigned to

The war is over! BA-10 armored cars stand in Viborg's center, the vehicles have no winter camoufl age and are painted in standard camoufl age colors, Mar. 13, 1940. (CAFM)

protect the airport in Luostari. To better the ground contact of the BT-5 tracks, the 86th Tank Battalion managed to fabricate and attach "dubs" to the feet of the tracks. With this procedure, it became possible for the tanks to maneuver even under conditions that prevailed north of the polar circle. During the entire war, the battalion lost only one BT-5, which was destroyed by an engine fire. On Dec 13, the 349th Special Tank Battalion was concentrated in the Petsamo area and placed at the 104th Rifle Division's disposal. That same day, a company of T-26's and a platoon of T-38's, assigned the mission of providing support to an offensive mounted by the 58th Rifle Regiment, advanced 48 kilometers into enemy territory.

On Dec 15, the battalion was concentrated in the Luostari area. From December 26 to March 13 a company of T-38's served duty by protecting the army's communications.

The 36th and 62nd Special Reconnaissance Battalions were used during the war to protect the army staff and the staff of the 52nd Rifle Division, as well as for liaison tasks.

To improve the ground surface grip of T-26 and T-37/38 tanks, sections of the track feet (each section consisting of anywhere from two to eight joined feet) were turned and re-coupled "inside-out." The results were positive.

The T-26 performed very successfully under conditions in the far north but the opposition it faced was not hard enough to test it fully.

Tank Force losses for the entire war period were: three T-26's due to artillery fire, two T-26's due to mine explosions, two T-26's due to sinking in water streams, and one BT-5 that burned in flames. Personnel losses mounted to four dead and five wounded.

A combat briefing of the tankers of the 20th Heavy Tank Brigade, November 30th, 1939. Note T-28 tanks in standard overall green camouflage pattern.

3:6 Home production for the front

Even as the war began, Leningrad's business firms were already taken up with meeting orders from the front: Many of these had never before engaged in production. The manufacturers in Leningrad – including those that worked directly for the defence department – experienced an acute shortage of electricity. As early as March 1939, at the XVIII Congress for VKP(b) (the Soviet Communist Party, the "Bolsheviks"), P. Popkov, one of Leningrad's leaders, stated, "For the last two years, Leningrad has suffered a shortage of energy." With the onset of war, this problem was further heightened. There wasn't sufficient coal – and in January, bread began to run out. Moreover, many men working for Leningrad businesses were called into the Red Army and this led to a shortage of qualified personnel. But despite such difficulties, as a whole, the manufacturers energetically tackled the work that had to get done in order to meet the needs at the front. As can be seen in the documentation of that period, the general population fully supported the Red Army's offensive against the "Finnish militarists."

In this section we will examine the various models of armored vehicles that were developed before the war and then used in combat and we'll also look at projects that were started based on the experience gained by personnel serving in armored vehicle units in battles at the Finnish front.

SMK and T-100 tanks

The heavy, double turreted SMK tanks (constructed at the Kirov Factory) and the T-100 tanks (constructed at Kirov Factory no. 185), began as projects in 1938 to replace the five-turreted T-35, and came to be tested on tank training grounds in the fall of 1939. When the war began, a decision was made to test them under actual field conditions. Both vehicles were supplied with crews, and on December 10, they were assigned to the 20th Heavy Tank Brigade. On December 19, during battle in the Summa-Hottinen district, an SMK – that had ventured deep into a Finnish installation – was exploded by a mine and abandoned by its crew.. The T-100 withdrew to its starting location and was subsequently shipped to the factory for routine repair. From February 22 to March 13, the T-100 returned and engaged in battle as part of the 20th and 1st Tank Brigades. During the war, Kirov Factory no.185 worked on an engineered-tank project based on

153

the T-100, and on a self-propelled 130 mm gun that could be used to attack bunkers. The latter, designated as the T-100U. ("Igrek") was set into production in February 1940, but wasn't available until after the war had ended. (More details about the SMK, T-100 and T-100U and their contribution in battle during the Soviet-Finnish War can be read in the "Frontillustration" publication no. 5, year 2005 – "Multi-turreted tanks with the RKKA/Red Army,ö.a./T-35,SMK and T-100.")

The KV tank

This tank began development at the Kirov factory parallel with the SMK. Originally, the KV was regarded as "having characteristics analogous to the SMK tank" but with only one turret and heavier armored plate. Therefore, The KV's turret was originally equipped with both a 76 and a 45 mm gun. In September 1939, the KV was tested on the proving grounds. When the war began, it was sent, together the SMK and the T-100, to the front. Subsequently, the 45 mm gun was replaced with a DT-19 type machine gun. On December 19, the KV heavy tank was accepted into the Red Army's arsenal. Meanwhile, at the same time, the Kirov Factory's design bureau received project request to install a 152 mm howitzer on a KV for attacking bunkers. In a very short time, the design engineers under the leadership of N. Kuron produced a considerably expanded turret containing a 152 mm M-17 howitzer. On February 17, a KV test model equipped with a 152 mm howitzer arrived at the front and became the first KV model to go into series production (factory number U-1). Before the war ended, two further KV tank examples arrived on the Karelian Isthmus: On February 22, a test-model KV (factory designation U-2) with a 76 mm gun mounted in the turret; and on February 29, a KV (factory designation U-3) with a 152 mm howitzer. All these tanks were combined, along with a T-100 tank, to form a special heavy tank company under the command of Captain Kolotusjkin. The company served with the 20th (from February 28 through March 1) and with the 1st (from March 1 to March 13) Tank Brigades. But when attacking bunkers, neither brigade used the KV tanks with 152 mm howitzers.

Tanks with reinforced armor plating

Leningrad's City Committee of the VKP(b) /the Soviet Union's Communist Party (the Bolsheviks), under the leadership A. Zjdanov, held a special meeting with the Military Council of the Lenin Military District (LVO). There, suggestions concerning ways of improving tanks were taken up. One of these advocated equipping tanks with extra thick – 30 to 40 mm – armored plating. And inasmuch as a T-26 model with reinforced armored plating – developed at Factory no. 174 under the direction of S, Ginzberg – had been successfully tested on December 30, a decision was made to immediately start producing such tanks. Factory no. 174 was given the job of reinforcing 27 T-26's, model 1939 and 27 ChT-133's – and the Kirov Factory the job of reinforcing 16 T-28's. The time it took to meet these orders, however, dragged on and it wasn't until the middle of February that these tanks reached the tank units. The first battles the tanks took part in revealed that Finnish anti-tank guns couldn't penetrate their reinforced armored plating. Therefore, another order was placed requesting reinforced armor for an additional 20 T-26's and 30 T-38's.

These tanks, however, didn't arrive at the front until the war was over and therefore came to be divided among the tank units after the war. In addition to the tanks just mentioned, a further 15 T-26, model 1939, tanks were reinforced at workshops in the city of Suojärvi (8th Army) by a work brigade from Factory no 174 (the Vorosjilov Factory)

Tank shields for the infantry

In December 1939, the production of protective apparatuses to be used by the infantry on the battlefield was organized at the Kirov and Izjorsk factories: tank shields (rounded disks) and Sokolov's sleds. In total, during the months of December 1939 and January 1940, 191 variously constructed tank shields on skies, and 250 examples of Sokolov's sleds were produced. The latter were set to be used for transport of infantry segments under fire and would be uncoupled and set free from the tank towing it when the enemy installation had been reached. The greater portion of this equipment was shipped to the Karelian Isthmus (all the tank sleds and 30,000 shields) but a share also went to the 8th and 15th Armies (appx. 3,000 shields). If properly used, they were very effective. For example, approximately 3,000 soldiers of the 8th and 15th Armies were duly instructed on the proper use of tank shields. During the advance towards Pitkäranta and the islands in the Ladoga that took place in March the shields proved to be: "fully usable … on smooth land as well as forest with a snow cover of up to 70cm. The rate of speed in the former case was 3 km/hr and in the second case, 1 km/hr, and when being fired upon by the enemy, 50-100 meters per hour." In order to increase the rate of speed, "for individual armored equipment to protect the infantry," a design group at the Kirov Factory led by K Kuzmin and L Syrjov carried out a project for the construction of a mobile machine gun nest (PPG or product 217). This vehicle was designed to support the infantry on the battlefield and represented a further development of tank sleds. It was armed with two machine guns and, powered by a motorcycle engine, it could propel itself over shorter distances. In combat situations, the crew would assume a prone position in the vehicle. As planned, a tank would tow the PPG to the battle field where it would then be released and used to protect the infantry from machine gun fire. The first model of this vehicle, however, was not completed until April 1940 (the factory at this time had an additional 5 examples under construction). But since the war had already ended, and given that this vehicle had been designed for use in a specific environment, its production was dropped.

Mine-sweepers for tanks.

In the early fighting, an acute need of various engineered equipment became apparent and first on line, stood mine sweepers. The manufacturers in Leningrad – the Kirov Factory, the Kirov Factory no. 185, and the Vorosjilov factory no. 174 – produced the first mine sweeper models in December 1939. In the beginning, these were simple constructions in the form of wood or metal plow-scrappers. The idea was that a tank would push such an attachment a safe distance before it and thereby set off any mines in its path. However, experience revealed that this simple construction was unreliable and needed further development. Some while later, a minesweeper utilizing discs was manufactured in series (91 were produced at the Kirov Factory, and 49 at the Vorosjilov factory no. 174). For the Soviet armies fighting in the Winter War, the sweepers became a part their equipment in February/March 1940. They were affixed to T-28's and T-26's and consisted of metal discs with a diameter of 700-900 cm, 10-25 mm thick mounted on a common axle. They weighed between 1,800 and 3,000 kilograms. Despite a weak tolerance to explosions (one explosion was enough to bend the discs), the mine-sweepers were successfully used by the 20th and 35th Tank Battalions and by the tank battalions of the 8th Army.

The Bridge tank

In order to get over anti-tank trenches, the Kirov Factory produced a 10 meter long, metal bridge securely mounted atop a T-28 tank. The intention was to have one such tank drive into the ditch and the other tanks would simply drive over the bridge. But tests revealed that this construction was ineffective and the project received no further attention.

The ambulance tank

In January 1940, at the request of soldiers and officers of the 35th Tank Brigade, Factory no. 174 started construction of a medical evacuation tank. This initiative was approved by the head of the Red Army's Armored Vehicle Command, D. Pavlov. Using the frame of an experimental A-1 tank as a platform (there were 8 such frames at the factory) and working directly on it, without engineering blueprints, a tank suitable for transporting the wounded was constructed. The factory's employees wanted to present this vehicle to the tank crews on their holiday, February 23 – Red Army Day. But due to production delays, there wasn't enough time for their ambulance tank to make it to the front.

Swedish volunteers inspecting a T37A at Pelkosenniemi in January 1940. Its former owners were the 177th Independent Recon batallion from the 122nd Infantry Division.

Three T-26 in the finnish workshops in Varkhaus after the end of the war in March 1940. From left to right, one can see one model 1931 and two model 1933.

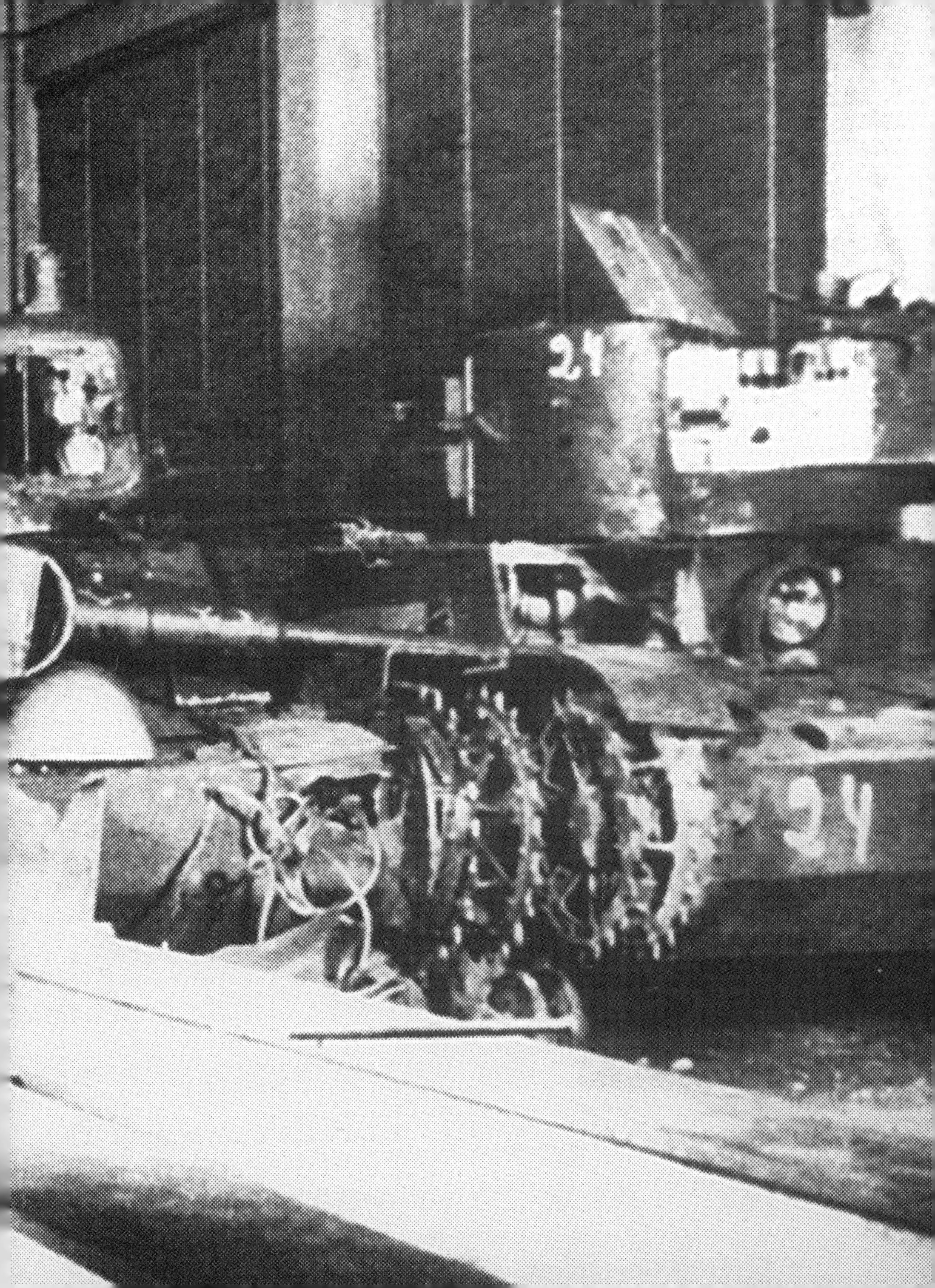

Appendix

4:1 Tank personnel who received the commendation "hero of the Soviet union" for their contribution in the Soviet-Finnish war

Araslanov, Gafijatulla Sjagimordanovitj – youngest commander, turret marksman in a tank company with the 136th Rifle Regiment, 97th Rifle Division.

Archipov, Vasilij Sergejevitj – Captain, company commander with the 35th Tank Brigade.

Baranov, Viktor Ilitj – Colonel, commander of the 13th Tank Brigade..

Bolesov, Ivan Egorovitj – youngest commander, mechanic/driver in the 62nd Tank Regiment.

Bragin, Nikolaj Michajlovitj – Political commander, tank battalion commissioner with the 20th Tank Brigade.

Butjakov, Sergej Nikolajevitj – youngest commander, tank commander in the 398th Special Tank Battalion with the 50th Rifle Division. (post humus).

Vinokurov, Boris Aleksandrovitj – Private, tank commander in the 398th Special Tank Battalion with the 50th Rifle Division.

Volk, Boris Vasilevitj – youngest commander, tank turret commander in the 20th Tank Battalion, (post humus)

Govorov, Sergej Aleksandrovitj – Lieutenant, company commander in the 13th Tank Brigade.

Gorsjkov, Jegor Gavrilovitj – youngest commander, mechanic/driver in a tank company with the 27th Rifle Regiment, 7th Rifle Division.

Gruzdev, Vasilij Grigorevitj – Lieutenant, platoon leader with the 20th Tank Brigade. (post humus)

Derjugin, Aleksej Vasilevitj – youngest commander, tank commander in the 35th Tank Brigade.

Didenko, Daniil Gavrilovitj – Warrant Officer, tank commander in the 35th Tank Battalion.

Dmitriev, Maksim Vasilevitj – Warrant Officer, mechanic/tank commander in 109th Special Intelligence Battalion, 86th Motorized Rifle Division.

Dudko, Fjodor Michajlovitj – Military Technician 1st Class, asst, commander in the 20th Tank Brigade's Technical unit. (post humus)

Djakonov, Jefrem Aristaulovitj – youngest commander, tank commander in a company with 27th Rifle Regiment, 7th Army Rifle Division.

Jevstratov, Nikolaj Aleksandrovitj – youngest military technician in the 20th Tank Brigade..

Jegorov, Konstantin Aleksandrovitj – 2nd Lieutenant, platoon leader in the 20th Tank Brigade. (post humus)

Jegorov, Michail Ivanovitj – asst. political commander, tank company commissioner with the 29th Tank Brigade.

Jezjov, Nikolaj Konstantinovitj – asst. platoon leader, tank commander in the 13th Tank Brigade, (post humus)

Jemeljanov, Ignat Dmitrievitj – Lieutenant, company commander in the 13th Tank Brigade. (post humus)

Zinin, Andrej Filippovitj – youngest commander, platoon leader in the 377th Special Tank Batallion, 97th Rifle Division..

Kasjuba, Vladimir Nesterovitj – Colonel, commander of the 35th Tank Brigade.

Kirpitjev, Illarion Pavlovitj – youngest commander, tank commander in the 13th Tank Brigade.

Kirjanov,. Pavel Nikolaevitj – Lieutenant, platoon leader in the 35th Tank Brigade..

Kitjigin, Nikolaj Grigorevitj – 2nd Lieutenant, platoon leader in the 40th Tank Brigade.

Klypin, Nikolaj Jakimovitj – 1st Lieutenant, chief-of-staff in the 62nd Tank Regiment.

Koval, Ivan Ivanovitj – Military Technician 2nd Class, technician in the 20th tank Brigade.

Kozlov, Viktor Dmitrievitj – youngest commander, tank commander in the 13th Tank Brigade.

Kolesso, Boris Adolfovitj – 1st Lieutenant, company commander in the 1st Tank Brigade. (post humus)

Komlev, Stepan Petrovitj – Lieutenant, company commander in the 20th Tank Brigade.

Krivoj, Evgenij Andreevitj – Private, turret marksman in the 35th Tank Brigade.

Krotov, Fjodor Fjodorovitj – youngest commander, mechanic/driver for the 35th Tank Brigade.

Krysjuk, Arsenij Pavlovitj – youngest commander, mechanic/driver for the 35th Tank Brigade.

.Kulabuchov, Valentin Fjodorovitj – 1st Lieutenant, company commander in the 35th Tank Brigade.

Kusjtin, Ivan Jakovlevitj – 2nd Lieutenant, platoon leader in the 1st Tank Brigade..

Lamzin, Fjodor Ivanovitj – Private, mechanic/driver in the 398th Special Tank Battalion, 50th Rifle Division. (post humus)

Lartjenko, Michail Andrejevitj – youngest commander, mechanic/driver for the 20th Tank Brigade.

Leljusjenko, Dmitrij Danilovitj – Colonel, commander of the 39th Tank Brigade.

Lichatjov, Vasilij Ivanovitj – Private, turret marksman in the 398th Special Tank Battalion, 50th Rifle Division. (post humus)

Lobastev, Michail Abramovitj – youngest commander, tank commander in the 20th Tank Brigade. (post humus)

Losjkov, Aleksej Ivanovitj – youngest commander, mechanic/driver for the 13th Tank Brigade.

Luppov, Evgenij Aleksejevitj – youngest commander, tank commander in the 20th Tank Brigade..

Makovskij, Iosif Isakovitj – Lieutenant, platoon leader in the 13th Tank Brigade.

Matvienko, Nikolaj Jefimovitj – youngest commander, platoon leader in the 307th Special Tank Battalion, 80th Rifle Division.

Masjkov, Nikolaj Vasilevitj – youngest commander, mechanic/driver in the 398th Special Tank Battalion. (post humus).

Nikolenko, Stepan Michajlovitj – 1st Lieutenant, battalion chief-of-staff in the 20th Tank Brigade.

Pavlov, Fjodor Pavlovitj – youngest commander, tank commander in the 35th Tank Brigade.

Pinjaev, Georgij Andrejevitj – Lieutenant, platoon leader in the 13th Tank Brigade.(post humus)

Pislegin, Viktor Kuzmitj – Private, turret marksman in the 62nd Tank Regiment.

Plotnikov, Aleksandr Grigorevitj – Lieutenant, platoon leader in the 28th Tank Regiment.

Prokofjev, Fjodor Vasilevitj – youngest commander, tank commander in the 28th Tank Regiment.

Prosjin, Ivan Ivanovitj – 1st Lieutenant, company commander in the 39th Tank Brigade.

Rozanov, Vasilij Petrovitj – 2nd Lieutenant, platoon leader in the 398th Special Tank Battalion, 50th Rifle Division. (post humus)

Rudakov, Evgenij Michajlovitj – Captain, company commander of the 394th Special Tank Battalion, 75th Rifle Division. (post humus)

Rudenjuk, Jakov Fjodorovitj – youngest commander, platoon leader in the 405th Special Tank Battalion, 7th Riffle Division..

Rusin, Nikita Ivanovitj – Private, mechanic/driver in the 39th Tank Battalion.

Samojlov, Ivan Arsenevitj – youngest commander, radio/telegraph operator in the 20th Tank Brigade.

Serebrjakov, Andrej Michajlovitj – youngest commander, mechanic/driver in the 39th Tank Brigade.

Sivolap, Ivan Danilovitj – youngest commander, mechanic/driver in the 40th Tank Brigade.

Simonjan, Karapet Semenovitj – Private, radio/telegraph operator for tanks in the 20th Tank Brigade.

Starkov, Georgij Veniaminovitj – 1st Lieutenant. Company commander in the 35th Tank Brigade.

Strjutjkov, Vasilij Vasilevitj – Private, mechanic/driver in the 398th Special Tank Battalion, 50th Rifle Division. (post-humus).

Sulaberidze, Aleksandr Sergejevitj – youngest crew-member, mechanic/driver for a tank company in the 27th Rifle Regiment, 7th Rifle Division.

Tarakanov, Aleksandr Jakovlevitj – 2nd Lieutenant, platoon leader in the 35th Tank Brigade.

Usjakov, Michail Filippovitj – Lieutenant, platoon leader in the 13th Tank Brigade

Frolov, Aleksandr Fjodorovitj – youngest commander, mechanic/driver in the 62nd Tank Regiment.

Chaprov, Ivan Vasilevitj – Private, turret marksman in the 35th Tank Brigade. (post-humus)

Haraborkin, Georgij Filimonovitj – 1st Lieutenant, company commander in the 20th Tank Brigade.

Tjepurenko, Anatolij Alekseevitj – Lieutenant, platoon leader in the 109th Special Intelligence Battalion, 86th Motorized Rifle Division

Tjistjakov, Michail Vasilevitj – youngest commander, tank commander in the 1st Tank Brigade..

Sjeronov, Leonid Vasilevitj – youngest crew-member, mechanic/driver in the 13th Tank Brigade.

Jurtjenko, Petr Fomitj –. Lieutenant, platoon leader in the 35th Tank Battalion

Jatnik, Sergej Fjodorovitj – Lieutenant, platoon leader in the 35th Tank Battalion

Hero of the Soviet Union, senior political officer of the 90th Tank Battalion, Politruk Bragin, February 1940.

A T37 being recovered by Finnish soldiers during the war

A T-26 model 1933 with damaged tracks on the Karelian Isthmus in 1940.

A Finnish collection point for Russian equipment. One can see a T-26, a artillery tractor and some GAZ cars.

A T-28M captured by the Finnish forces in Karelia

4:2 Vehicle facts appendix with pictures

T-26 model 1931-1932

This was the most common light tank in the Red army before 1941. It was designed for the purpose of fighting enemy infantry and it´s main targets were supposed to be enemy machineguns, and the general idea was that it shouldn´t have anything to fear from enemy tanks. In practice this turned out to be the designs greatest flaw.. As basis for the tank, the Vickers-Armstrong-chassi, were used. That was the same chassi as used in the Vickers tank that Finland bought during the 1930s and that the T-26 were in combat with during the Winterwar. The tanks speed were low, the protection only sufficient against machine guns, but it´s armament were good. In total over 11 000 examples of the design were produced.

Production period: 1931-33
Tonnage: 8,7 tonnes
Crew: 3
Length: 4,62 meters
Width: 2,44 meters
Height: 2,19 meters
Ground clearence: 38 cm

Engine: 4-cylinders T-26 gasoline engine
Engine capacity: 90 HP at 2000rpm
Fuel capacity: 180 liters
Maximum speed: 28 kph
Maximum range: 160 km

Armament: 2x DT 7,62mm machine gun
alternative: 1x 37mm PS-1 gun
1x DT 7,62mm machine gun
Ammunition quantity: 6600 rounds
alternative: 222 shells and 3500 rounds
Armour thickness: 6-15mm

T-26 model 1933-1938

Production period: 1933-38
Tonnage: 9,5 tonnes
Crew: 3
Length: 4,62 meters
Width: 2,44 meters
Height: 2,22 meters
Ground clearence: 38 cm

Engine: 4-cylinders T-26 gasoline engine
Engine capacity: 90 hp vid 2000rpm
Fuel capacity: 285 liters
Maximum speed: 28 kph
Maximum range: 375 km
Armament: 1x 45mm 20K gun
1-2x DT 7,62mm machine guns

Ammunition quantity: 122 shells and 3500 rounds
Armour thickness: 10-15mm

T-26 model 1939

Production period: 1938-41
Tonnage: 10,2 tonnes
Crew: 3
Length: 4,62 meters
Width: 2,44 meters
Height: 2,33 meters
Ground clearence: 38 cm

Engine: 4-cylinders T-26 gasoline engine
Engine capacity: 100 hp vid 2200rpm
Fuel capacity: 292 liters
Maximum speed: 30 kph
Maximum range: 220 km

Armament: 1x 45mm 20K gun
1-2x DT 7,62mm machine guns
Ammunition quantity: 140-180 shells and 3500 rounds
Armour thickness: 10-20mm

T-28 model 1932

Sovjets first mediumweight tank in seriesproduction. Designed according to the pre-warconcept of "landcruisers". The basics of the concept were that the tanks should be able to perform more than one task and therefore had a variety of weaponry, and be looked upon as ships on land, or cruisers on land. The big drawback with the concept and this design, were that most tanks of the 1930s lacked radio communications and had very bad internal communication equipement in the tanks, and this meant that the members of the crew most of the times had to make their own decisions of what to do and in what order. Therefore the advantage of fighting several targets at the same time, became a big disadvantage. Add to this the tank´s bad protection and low speed and he final result was not godd at all. In total 503 examples were built.

Production period: 1933-37
Tonnage: 25,2 tonnes
Crew: 6
Length: 7,44 meters
Width: 2,87 meters
Height: 2,82 meters
Ground clearence: 56 cm

Engine: 12-cylinders M-17L gasoline engine
Engine capacity: 500 hp vid 1500 rpm
Fuel capacity: 650 liters
Maximum speed: 40 kph
Maximum range: 220 km

Armament: 1x 76,2mm M27/32 gun
3-4x 7,62mm DT machine guns
Ammunition quantity: 64-70 shells and 8000 rounds
Armour thickness: 10-30mm

T-28 M

Production period: 1937-40
Tonnage: 32 tonnes
Crew: 6
Length: 7,44 meters
Width: 2,87 meters
Height: 2,82 meters
Ground clearence: 56 cm

Engine: 12-cylinders M-17L gasoline engine
Engine capacity: 500 hp vid 1500 rpm
Fuel capacity: 650 liters
Maximum speed: 23 kph
Maximum range: 180 km

Armament: 1x 76,2mm L-10 gun
3-4 7,62mm DT machine guns
Ammunition quantity: 69 shells and 8000 rounds
Armour thickness: 10-80mm

T-35

The ultimate "landcruiser" design. A battleship on land. With a armament of 3 guns and up to 6 machineguns. Entered production 1932 and was designed after the French models in existence at the time. The armament made it possible to möjliggjorde bekämpning av flera stridsvagnar samt infanterimål samtidigt. This colossus had a far to weak engine and very poor protection. Most of the tanks became losses when the engine simply broke down. Only 62 were built during 7 years.

Production period: 1932-39
Tonnage: 45 tonnes
Crew: 10
Length: 9,72 meters
Width: 3,2 meters
Height: 3,43 meters
Ground clearence: 53 cm

Engine: 12-cylinders M-17M gasoline engine
Engine capacity: 500 hp vid 1500 rpm
Fuel capacity: 910 liters
Maximum speed: 30 kph
Maximum range: 150 km
Armament: 1x 76,2mm M27/32 gun

2x 45mm M34 guns
5-6 7,62mm DT machine guns
Ammunition quantity:
96-100x 76,2mm shells
220-226x 45mm shells
9-10000x 7,62mm rounds
Armour thickness: 11-30mm

BT-2

One of the fastest tanks in the world at the outbreak of the war. The BT were designed to act as a cavalry-tank or as a brekthrough-tank, both missions required high speed to be able to exploit a breakthrough and wreak havoc behind enemy lines. The basis of the tank, were the Christie design, the same as for the T-34. This meant that it could be driven both on tracks and on the wheels. This gave of course, a much higher possible speed, which was the general idea. It had, for it´s time, a very strong engine and good armament, but the protection were not sufficient. In total, some 8000 examples of all models, were built until 1940.

Production period: 1931-33
Tonnage: 11,3 tonnes
Crew: 2-3
Length: 5,7 meters
Width: 2,23 meters
Height: 2,28 meters
Ground clearence: 36,5 cm

Engine: 12-cylinders Liberty gasoline engine
Engine capacity: 343 hp vid 2000 rpm
Fuel capacity: 400 liters
Maximum speed: wheels: 110 kph, tracks: 62 kph
Maximum range: wheels: 300 km, tracks: 200 km

Armament: 1x 37mm BS-3 gun
1-2x 7,62mm DT machine guns
Alt: 3x 7,62mm DT machine guns
Ammunition quantity:
96 shells and 2700 rounds
Alt: 6000 rounds
Armour thickness: 6-13mm

BT-5

Production period: 1933-37
Tonnage: 11,5 ton
Crew: 3
Length: 5,7 meter
Width: 2,23 meter
Height: 2,28 meter
Ground clearence: 36,5 cm

Engine: 12-cylinders M-5 gasoline engine
Engine capacity: 350 hp vid 2300 rpm
Fuel capacity: 400 liter
Maximum speed: wheels: 72 kph, tracks: 52 kph
Maximum range: wheels: 300 km, tracks: 200 km

Armament: 1x 45mm M-32 gun
1-2x 7,62mm DT machine guns
Ammunition quantity:
72-115 shells and 2700 rounds
Armour thickness: 6-13mm

BT-7

Production period: 1934-40
Tonnage: 13,8 tonnes
Crew: 3
Length: 5,7 meters
Width: 2,23 meters
Height: 2,40 meters
Ground clearence: 42 cm

Engine: 12-cylinders M-15T gasoline engine
Engine capacity: 450 hp vid 1700 rpm
Fuel capacity: 790 liter
Maximum speed: wheels: 73 kph, tracks: 53 kph

Maximum range: wheels: 500 km, tracks: 375 km
Armament: 1x 45mm M-34 gun
2-3x 7,62mm DT machine guns
Ammunition quantity: 132-188 shells and 2700 rounds
Armour thickness: 6-22mm

T-27

The first light tank in the Soviet arsenal to enter series production, was in reality a so called tankette. The design were based on the Brittish design Carden-Lloyd. It had only a grew of 2, a weak engine and weak protection, so it was never considered a success, as a light tank. It was mainly used as a reconnaissance tank. In total 2500 were built.

Production period: 1931-33
Tonnage: 2,7 tonnes
Crew: 2
Length: 2,6 meters
Width: 1,63 meters
Height: 1,44 meters
Ground clearence: 24 cm

Engine: 4-cylinders GAZ-AA gasoline engine
Engine capacity: 40 hp vid 2200 rpm
Fuel capacity: 46 liters
Maximum speed: 40 kph
Maximum range: 120 km

Armament:
1x DT machine gun 7,62mm
Ammunition quantity: 2500 rounds
Armour thickness: 4-10 mm

T-37A

This was Soviets first real amphibious tank. The design were based on the Brittish Carden-Lloyd, just as the T27 were. This tank had a fully revolving turret armed with a machine gun.

It was fully amphibious but had low protection. It was only used for reconnaissance. In total some 2200 were made.

Production period: 1933-36
Tonnage: 3,2 tonnes
Crew: 2
Length: 3,75 meters
Width: 2 meters
Height: 1,82 meters
Ground clearence: 30 cm

Engine: 4-cylinders GAZ-AA gasoline engine
Engine capacity: 40 hp vid 2200 rpm
Fuel capacity: 100 liters
Maximum speed: 36 kph on land, 4-6 kph in water
Maximum range: 230 km

Armament: 1x DT machine gun 7,62mm
Ammunition quantity: 585 rounds
Armour thickness: 6-9 mm

T-38M2

The T38M2 were a modified T-37, but could also be called a new design. It had a stronger engine than it´s predecessor, reached higher speeds, but still had the same basic problem as it´s predecessor, weak protection and armament, which meant that it hardly was efficient in it´s intended capacity as a reconnaissance tank. 1300 were made.

Production period: 1936-39
Tonnage: 3,8 tonnes
Crew: 2
Length: 3,75 meters
Width: 2,33 meters
Height: 1,63 meters
Ground clearence: 30 cm

Engine: 4-cylinders GAZ-M1 gasoline engine
Engine capacity: 50 hp vid 2800 rpm
Fuel capacity: 100 liters
Maximum speed: on land: 46 kph, in water: 6 kph

Maximum range: 230 km
Armament:
1x DT machine gun 7,62mm
Ammunition quantity: 1500 rounds
Armour thickness: 6-9mm

BA-27

Sovjet´s first design of a heavy armoured car. It were designed already in 1927, and it is considered the predecessor of the BA-10. It had weak protection but was the first armoured car of it´s time to be armed with a gun bigger than a machine gun. The gun were in a fully revolving turret. But the weak element of the design were the 6x4 drive. Only ca 200 examples were built.

Production period: 1927-31
Tonnage: 4,4 tonnes
Crew: 4
Length: 4,62 meters
Width: 1,71 meters
Height: 2,52 meters
Ground clearence: 24,5 cm

Engine: AMO gasoline engine
Engine capacity: 52 hp vid 2500 rpm
Fuel capacity: 88 liters
Maximum speed: 45 kph
Maximum range: 200 km
Armament: 1x 37mm gun
   1x DT 7,62mm machine gun

Ammunition quantity:
37mm – 40 shells
7,62 mm 2000 rounds
Armour thickness: 3-8 mm

BA-10

The most common armoured car in the Soviet inventory during the war years 1939 – 1945. It had a 45 mm gun in it´s turret and one machine gun, and therefore it was classified as sufficently armed for it´s time. It also had good protection for it´s time. The big drawback was it´s 6x4 drive, as that meant low cross-terrain capacity. In total 3300 were made during the war years.

Production period: 1937-42
Tonnage: 5 tonnes
Crew: 4
Length: 4,66 meters
Width: 2,07 meters
Height: 2,21 meters
Ground clearence: 22 cm

Engine: GAZ-M1 Diesel engine
Engine capacity: 52 hp vid 2800 rpm
Fuel capacity: 120 liters
Maximum speed: 53 kph
Maximum range: 250 km
Armament: 1x 45mm M1938
   2x DT machine guns 7,62mm

Ammunition quantity:
45mm – 43 shells
7,62mm 2100 rounds
Armour thickness: 10-15mm

D-8/D-12

The first light armoured car design in the Red army inventory during the 1930s. High speed but no turret, and that meant that the design were dropped after only 60 examples had been produced. The Finnish army used it as a staff vehicle.

Production period: 1932-33
Tonnage: 1,6 tonnes
Crew: 2
Length: 3,54 meters
Width: 1,70 meters
Height: 1,90 meters
Ground clearence: 22 cm

Engine: Ford-A gasoline engine
Engine capacity: 40 hp vid 2500 rpm
Fuel capacity: 40 liters
Maximum speed: 85 kph
Maximum range: 225 km
Armament: 1x DT 7,62mm machine gun
Ammunition quantity: 2700 rounds

Armour thickness: 3-7 mm

BA20/FAI

Another early Soviet armoured car design. 4x4 drive. One machinegun in a fully revolving turret. Weak protection but high speed.
697 examples were built in total.

Production period: 1934-36
Tonnage: 2 tonnes
Crew: 3
Length: 4 meters
Width: 1,80 meters
Height: 2,05 meters
Ground clearence: 19 cm

Engine: GAZ M-1 gasoline engine
Engine capacity: 50 hp vid 2800 rpm
Fuel capacity: 60 liters
Maximum speed: 80 kph
Maximum range: 250 km
Armament: 1x DT 7,62mm machine gun
Ammunition quantity: 1500 rounds

Armour thickness: 3-6 mm

4:3 Literature and sources

1. Rossijskij gosudarstvennyj voennyj archive.
   Fondy: Avtobronetankovoje upravlenije RKKA, Glavnoje artillerijskoje upravlenije RKKA, Sekretariat narkoma oborony SSSR, Kollektsija materialov po sovjetsko-finljandskoj vojne, Sjtab Leningradskogo vojennogo okruga.
2. Rossijskij gosudarstvennyj economic achive.
   Fondy: Ministerstvo tjazjologo masjinostroenija SSSR, 3-e Glavnoe upravlenije narkomata tankovoj promysjlennosti.
3. Tajny i uroki zimnej vojny. – SPB: «Poligon», 2000. – 544 s.
4. Zimnjaja vojna 1939 –1940. Kniga 1. Polititjeskaja istorija. – M: «Nauka», 1999. – 384 s.
5. Zimnjaja vojna 1939 –1940. Kniga 2. I.V. Stalin i finskaja kampanija. – M: «Nauka», 1999. – 305 s.
6. Boi v Finljandii (vospominanija utjastnikov), tjast I i II. – M: Voennoje izdatelstvo Narodnogo Komissariata Oborony Sojuza SSR, 1941. – 392 i 408 s.
7. Manninen O. Neuvostoliiton operatiiviset suunnitelmat Suomen suunnalla, 1939-1941. Sotahistoriallinen Aikakauskirja. Yväskylä, 1993. Osa II.
8. Esa Muikku, Jukka Purhonen. The Finnish Armoured Vehicles 1918-1997. Apali OY, Tampere, 1998.

4:4 Maps and tank illustrations

At the beginning of the war, the main portion of Finland's military might was located on the Karelian Isthmus. Altogether, there were six divisions split between two army corps. A third army corps, consisting of two divisions, was located north of Lake Ladoga

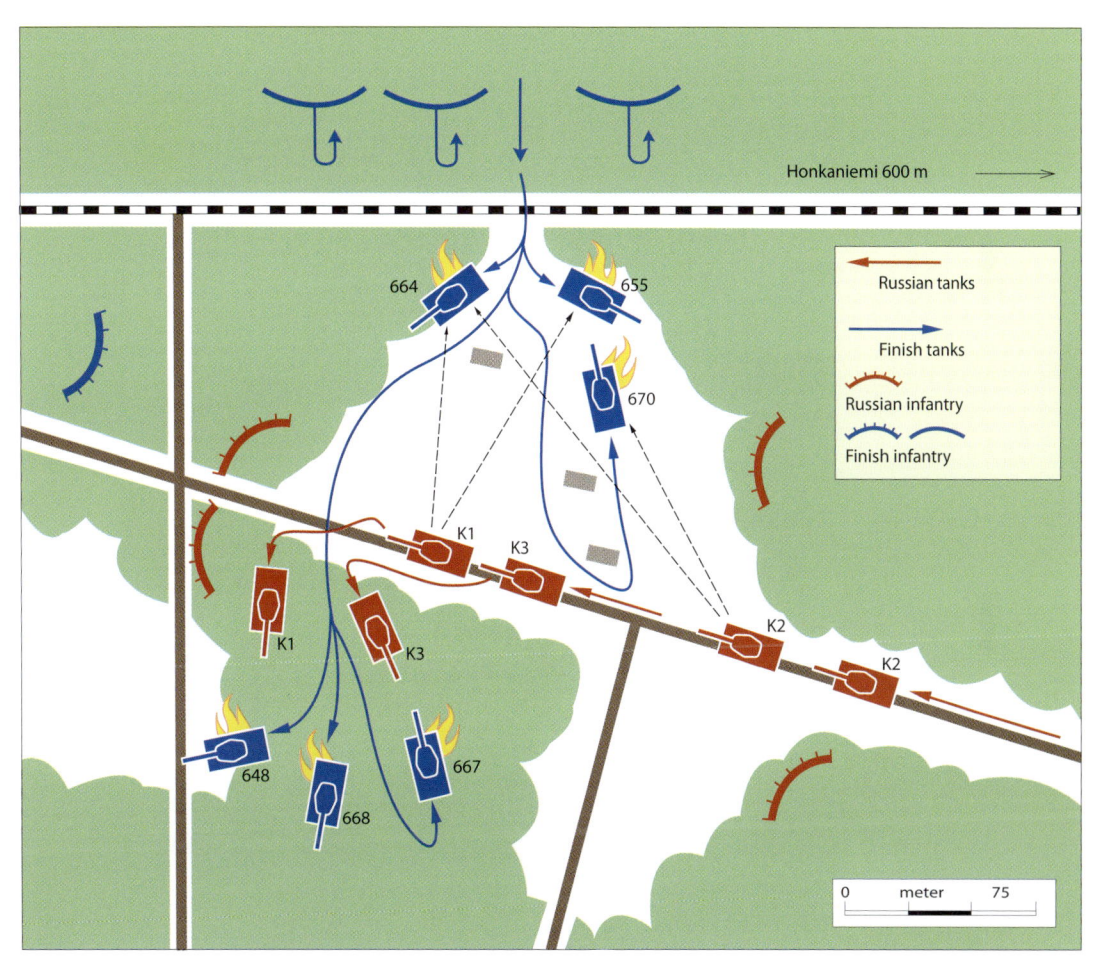

Map-sketch of the battles at Honkaniemi on februari 26 1940.

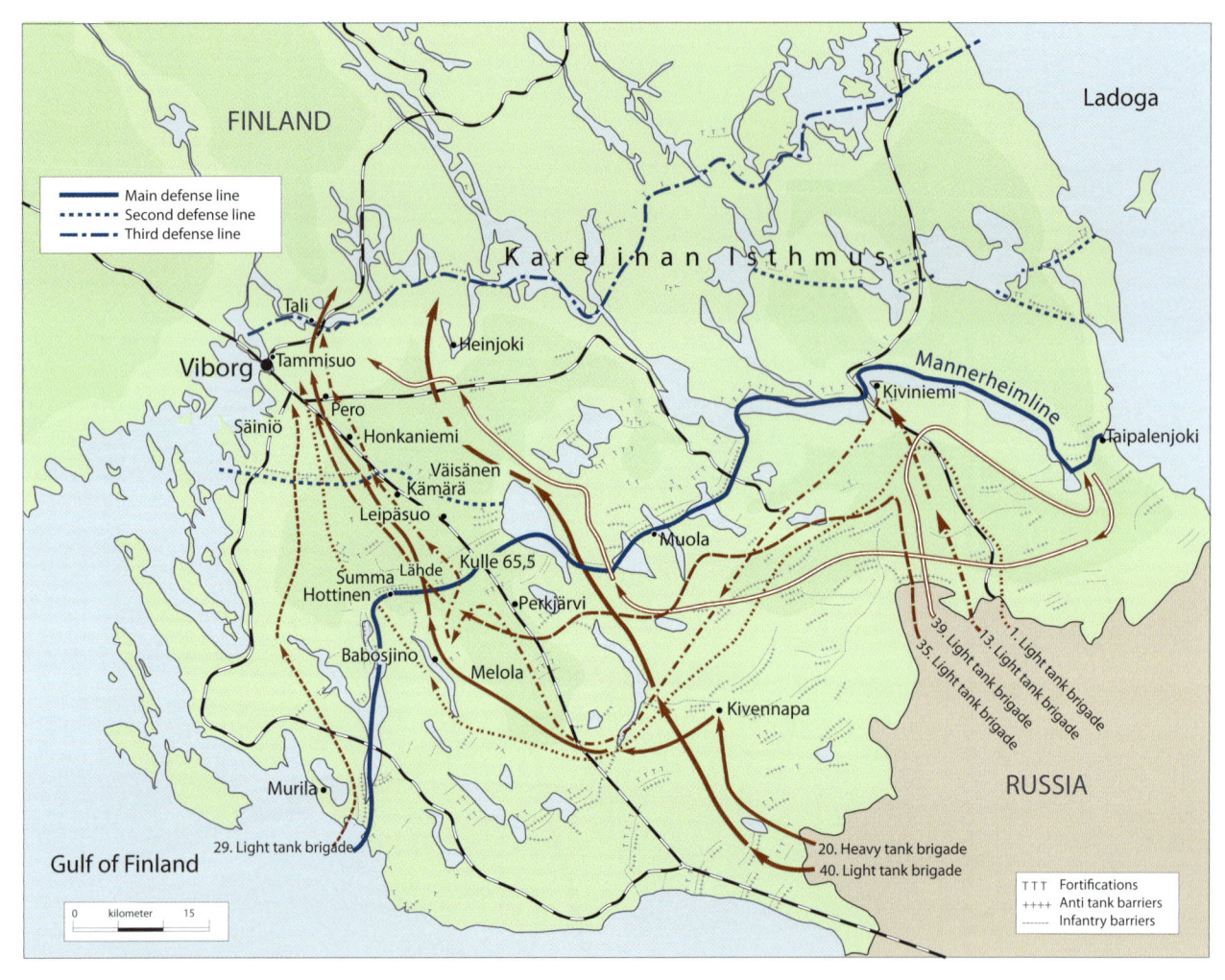

Map-sketch of the Red Army's tank brigades on the Karelian Isthmus from November 30 1939 to March 13, 1940

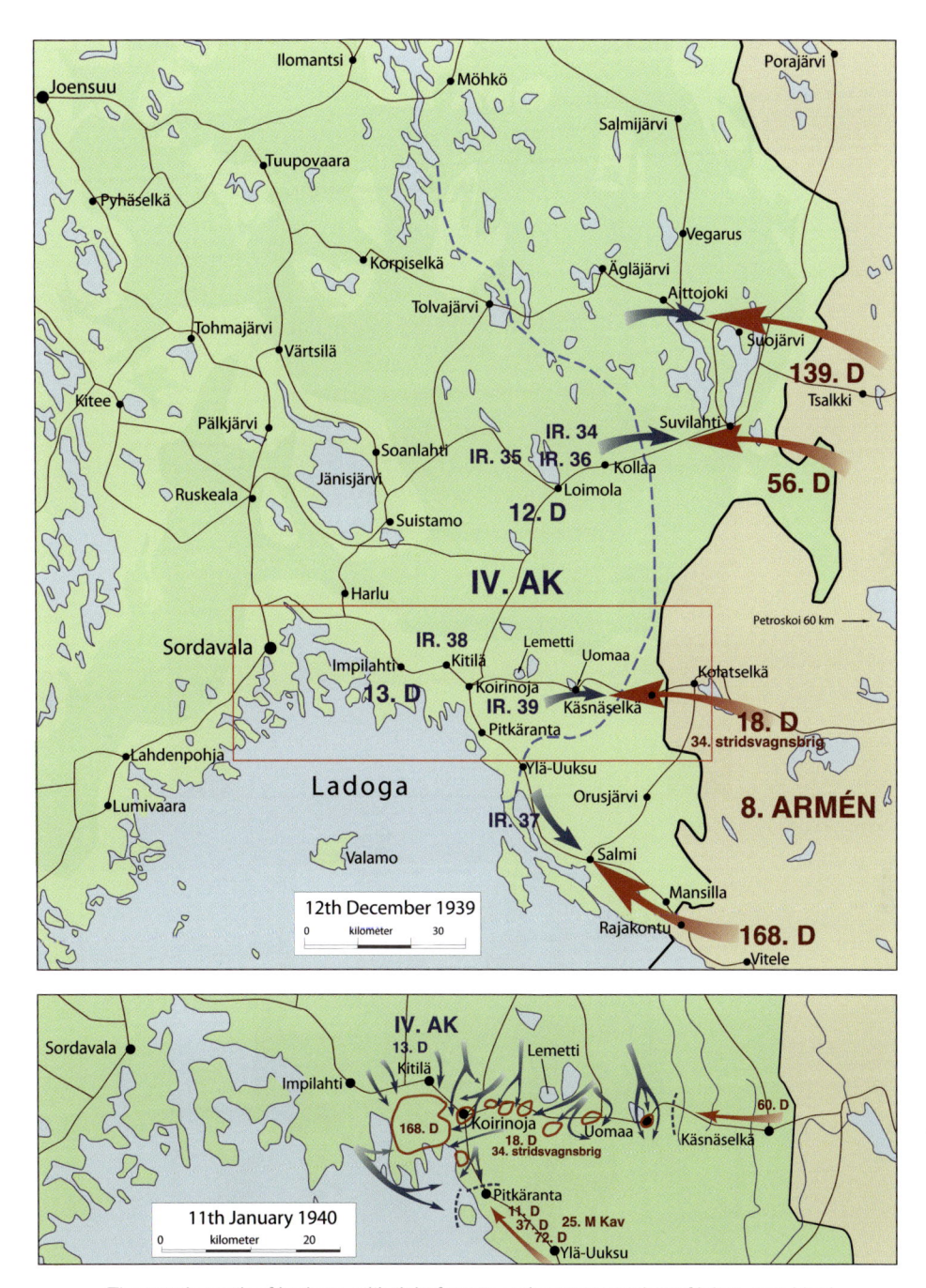

The terrain north of Ladoga, with tight forests and a great number of lakes, was ideal for defensive warfare. The Soviet's 18th Division was totally annihilated by Finnish attacks, and the 168th Division was a hair's-breadth from meeting the same fate.

A BT-5 from one of the Light Tank brigades on the Karelian Isthmus 1940.

A T-27 tankette from the 123rd Rifle Division, December 1939

A T-38 Amphibious tank somewhere in Karelia November 1939,

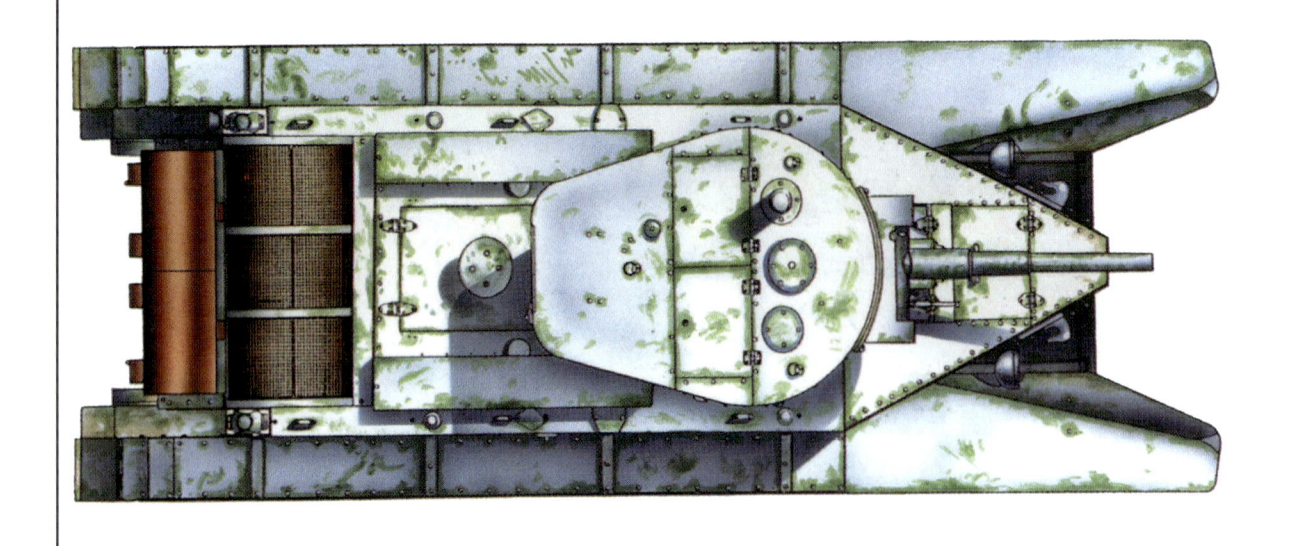

A T-37A from the 79th Independent Tank battalion in the 9th Army, December 1939.

A BT-5 from one of the Light Tank brigades on the Karelian Isthmus 1940.

A T-26 model 1931 somewhere in Karelia January 1940.

A T-35 model 1936 from one of the Heavy Tank brigades on the Karelian Isthmus in February 1940.

A T-26 model 1933 on the Karelian Isthmus 1940.

A T-26 model 1933 on the Karelian Isthmus 1940.

T-38 amphibious tank from the 18th Recce Battalion of the 13th Army, Karelian Isthmus, January 1940.

Prototype of model SMK belonging to the 20th Heavy Tank Brigade, Karelian Isthmus, December 1939.

T-37A amphibious tank from 177th Independent Recce Battalion, 122nd Rifle Division, December 1939.

T-28 tank of the 90th Tank Battalion 20th Heavy Tank Brigade, Karelian Isthmus, January-February 1940.

A FAI-M Armoured car from a unidentified unit, February 1940.

A T-28 from the 20th Tank brigade on the Karelian Isthmus, February 1940.

Type T-28 tank from the 20th Heavy Tank Brigade, Karelian Isthmus, February 1940. The tactical marker of the 90th Tank Battalion – a square, outlined and divided in the middle in red – can be seen on the side of the tank.

Radio-controlled, type T-26 tank from the 17th Special Chemical Tank Brigade. This tank was destroyed by the enemy in the area of height 65.5, near the Mannerheim Line in January 1940. The tank was not painted in white and still remains in the green/brown camouflage suitable for fall.

The turret. Uncertain as to which tank unit this tank belonged. Note the carelessly applied white paint, possible a so-called "whitewash" – much of which had already worn or washed away. (Ill. Maarten Swarts)

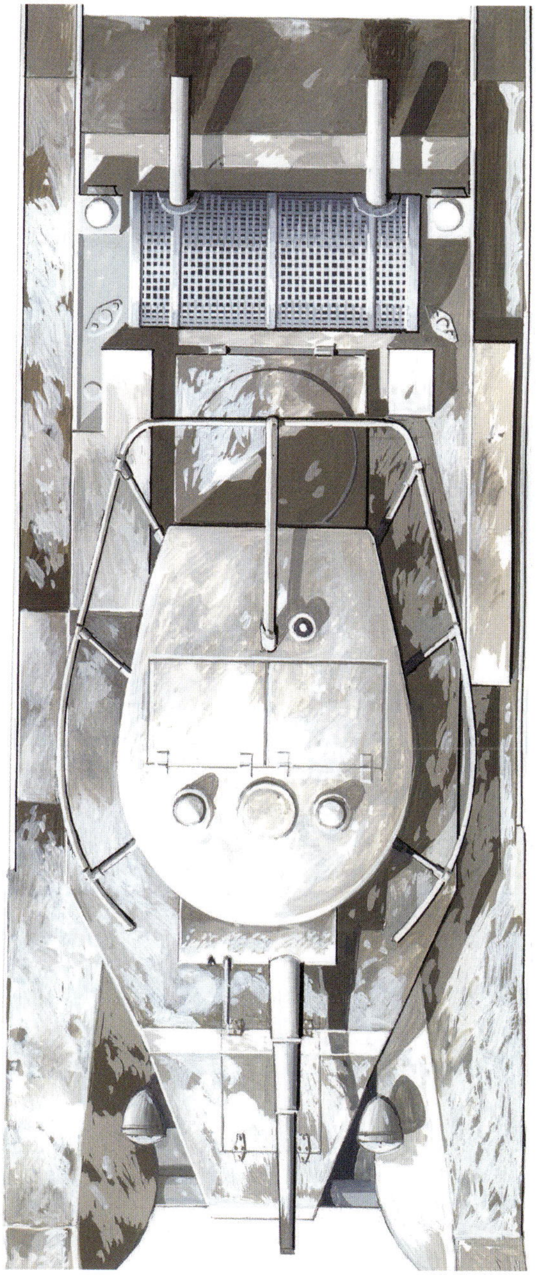

Type T-26 tank, model 1939, in winter camouflage. Probably belonging to the 40th Light Tank Brigade, Karelian Isthmus, February 1940. Only the upper body and turret are painted white. The tactical marking, formed as "00" in red, is visible on the turret's side. The turret's hatch is not painted white, making the tank easier to identify from the air, and a tarp and a bundle of logs, useful for getting over anti-tank moats, have been secured on the tank's stern.

Type T-37 tank from the Special Tank Battalion, 163rd Rifle Division, 9th Army Zone, December 1939.

Type FT-17 Renault, a Finnish tank from the 2nd Tank Company. This tank was captured by the Red Army in the vicinity of the Pero railway station in February 1940. Above the tri-colored camoufl age application, someone has laid on white with wide brush strokes. Its tactical number "4" is visible on the turret and on the stern can be seen the 2nd Company's insignia – a red hourglass??? in a white circle.

Type BT-7 tank "For Stalin" Northwest Front, artillery squad in the 13th Light Tank Brigade, February 1939.

Type BT-7 tank (with conical turret) out of the 13th Light Tank Brigade, Karelian Isthmus, January 1940.

Type ChT-26 tank out of the 210th Special Chemical Tank Battalion, Karelian Isthmus, January 1940. Its tactical number is visible on the turret – 3/2.

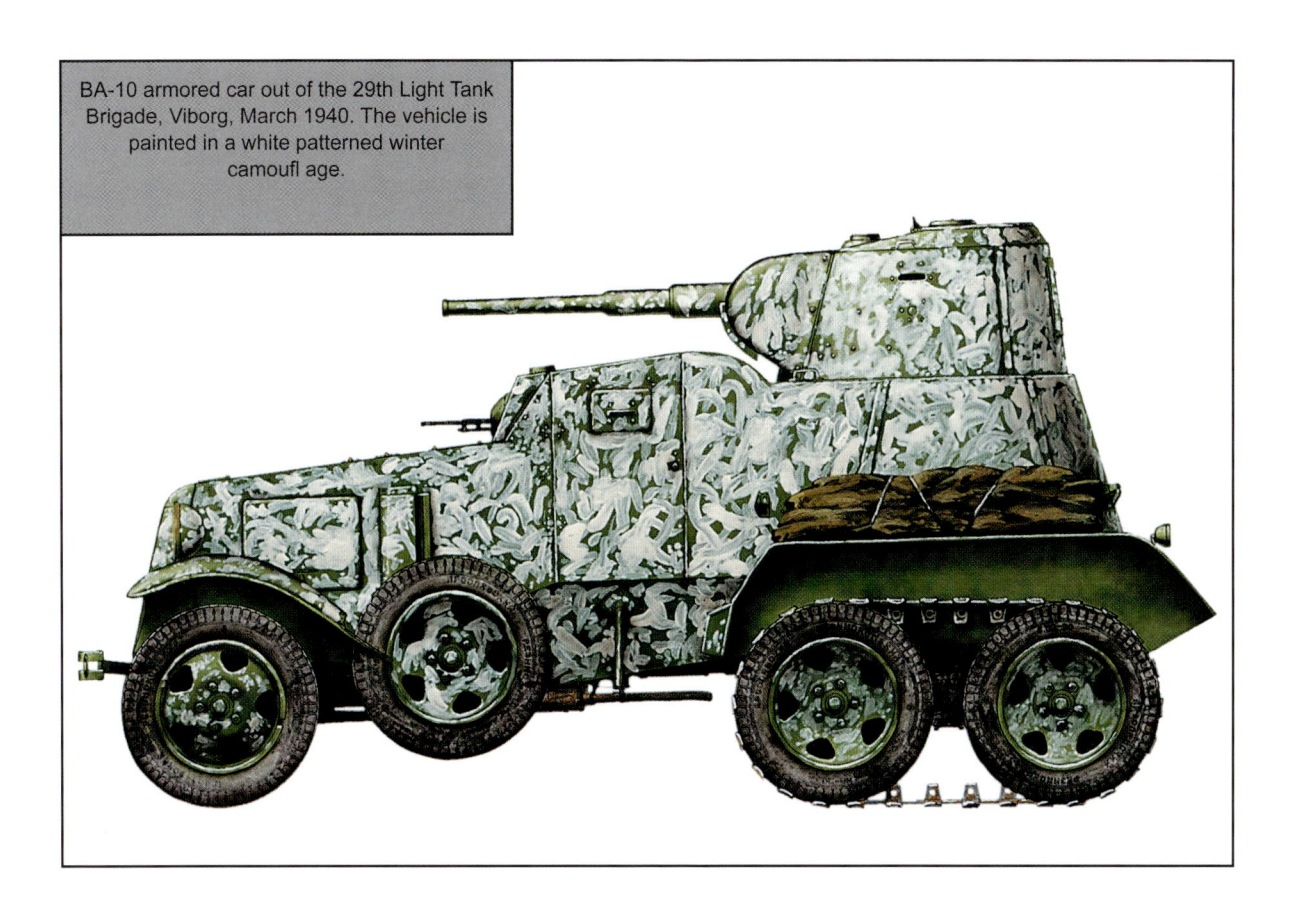

BA-10 armored car out of the 29th Light Tank Brigade, Viborg, March 1940. The vehicle is painted in a white patterned winter camoufl age.

Self-propelled 76 mm Kurtjevskij anti-tank gun on a type GAZ-TK truck (SPK), 9th Army Zone, 4th Special Intelligence Battalion in the 44t Rifle Division, February 1940.

T-26, model 1931, possibly belonging to the 377th Independent Tank Battalion, Karelian Isthmus, winter of 1939-40.

One of the armoured cars captured by the Finns – model BA-20M, Karelian Isthmus, March 1940.

BT-7, model 1939, belonging to the 13th Light Tank Brigade, 10th Tank Corp on the Karelian Isthmus, December 1939.

T-28, model 1938, belonging to the 20th Heavy Tank Brigade, Karelian Isthmus, January 1940.

BT-5 out of the 34th Light Tank Brigade, middle south Lemetti, February 1940.

Amphibious-tank captured by the Finns, model T-38M2, at the Varkhaus workshop, spring of 1940.

KhT-26 chemical tank captured by the Finns, Varkhaus workshop, spring of 1940.

Prototype of model SMK belonging to the 20th Heavy Tank Brigade, Karelian Isthmus, December 1939.

203

T-28 from the 29th Brigade, February 1940. Note that the entire tank had been painted white – Note too that much of this paint has worn off in a number of places

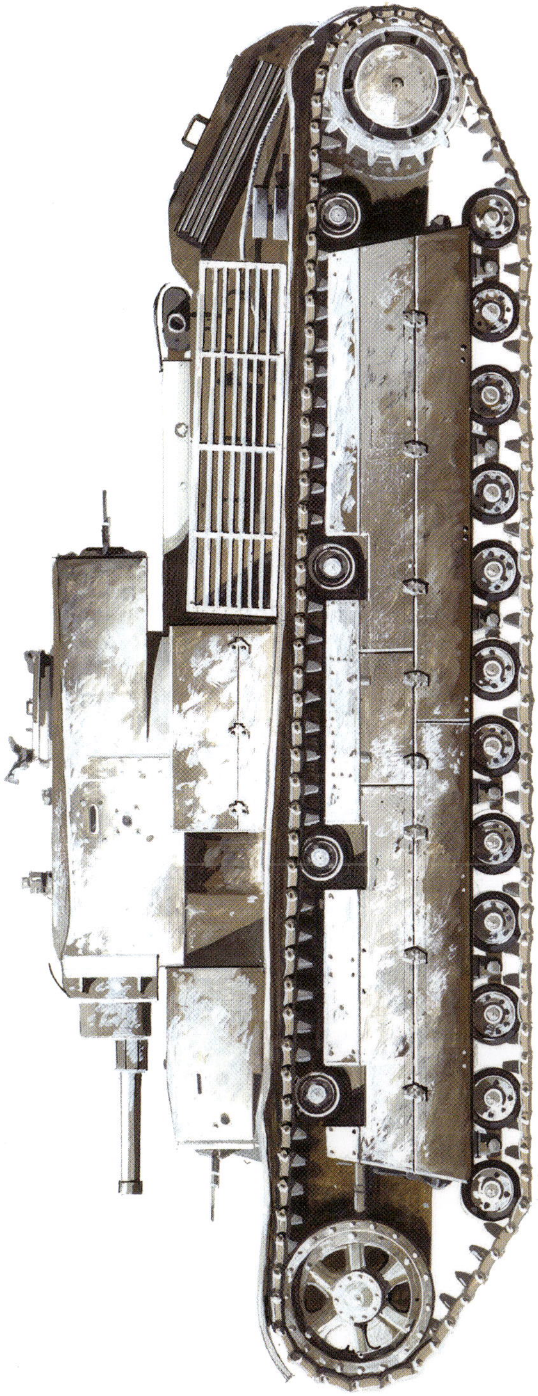

T-28 from the 29th Brigade, February 1940. Note that the entire tank had been painted white – Note too that much of this paint has worn off in a number of places

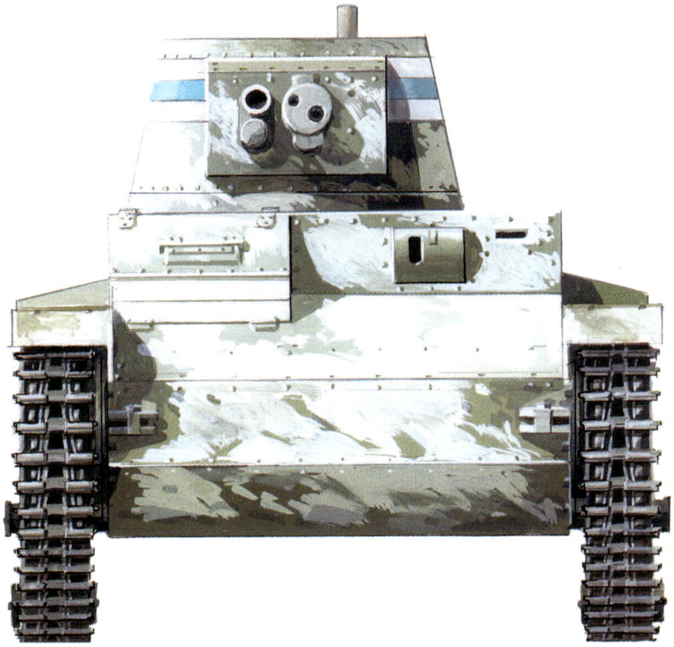

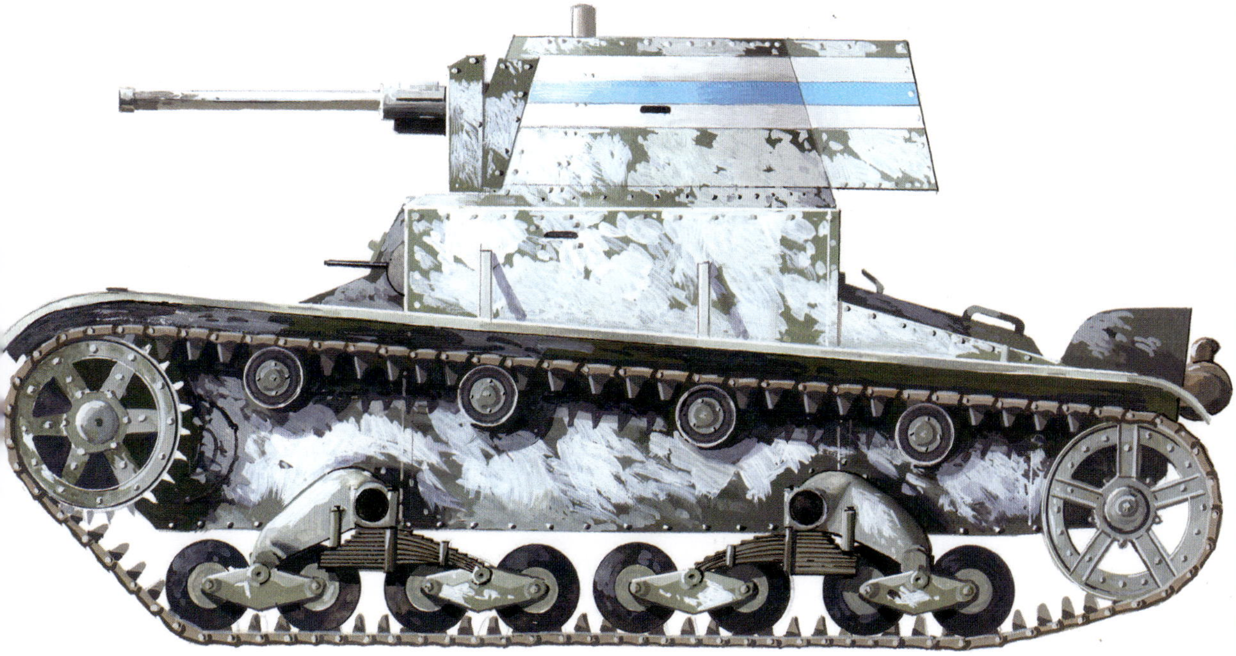

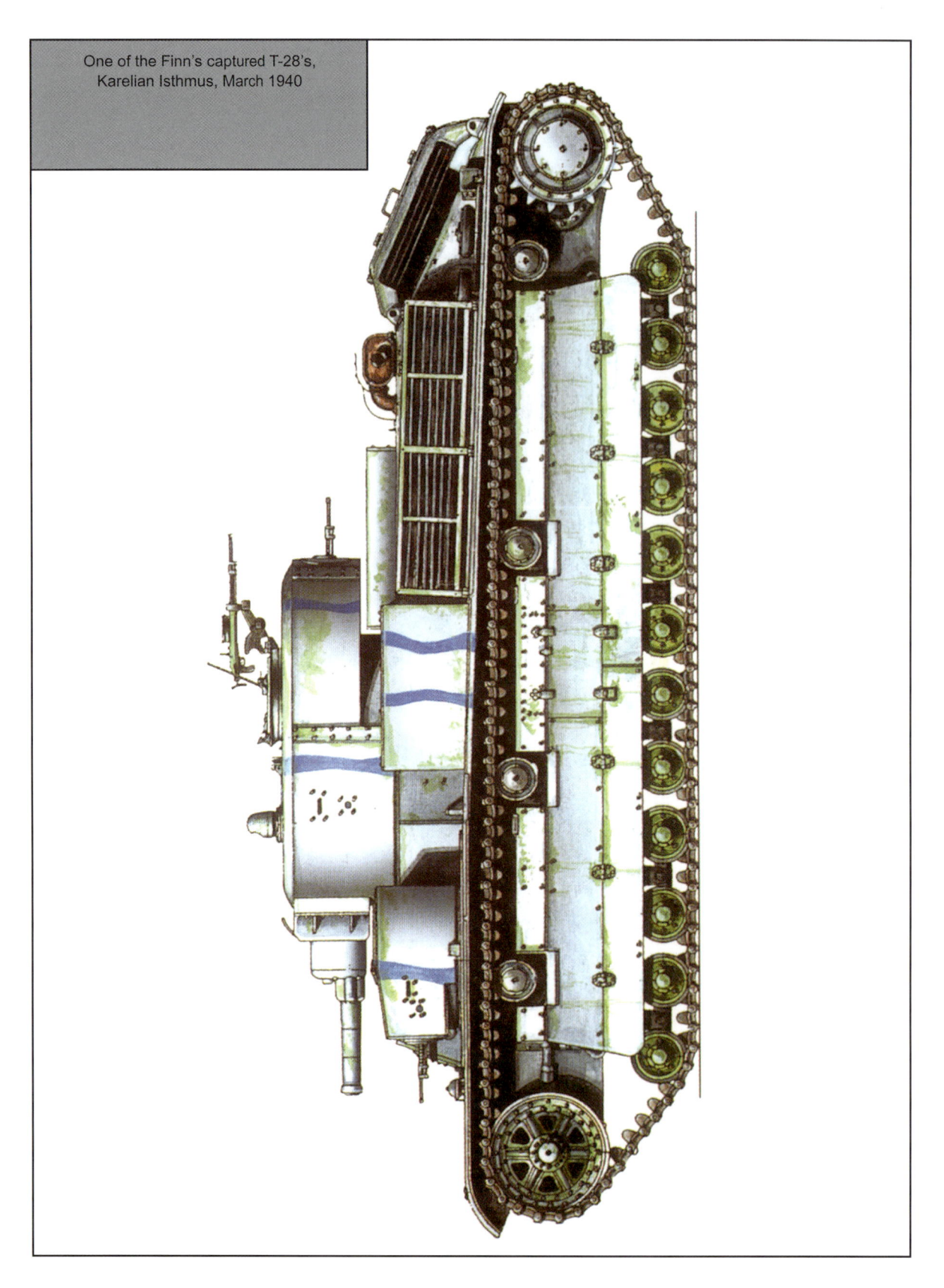

One of the Finn's captured T-28's, Karelian Isthmus, March 1940

4:5 Blueprints

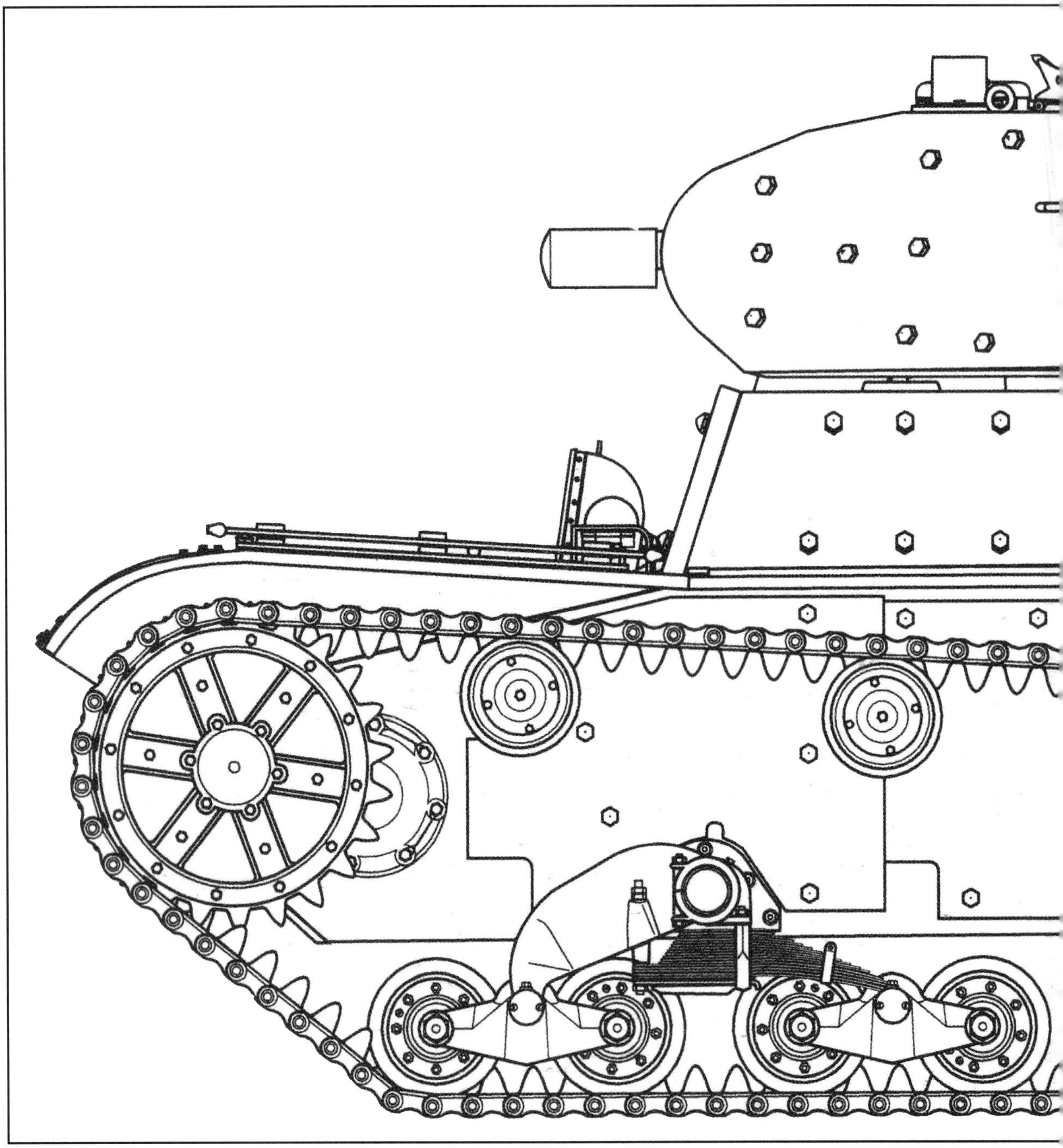

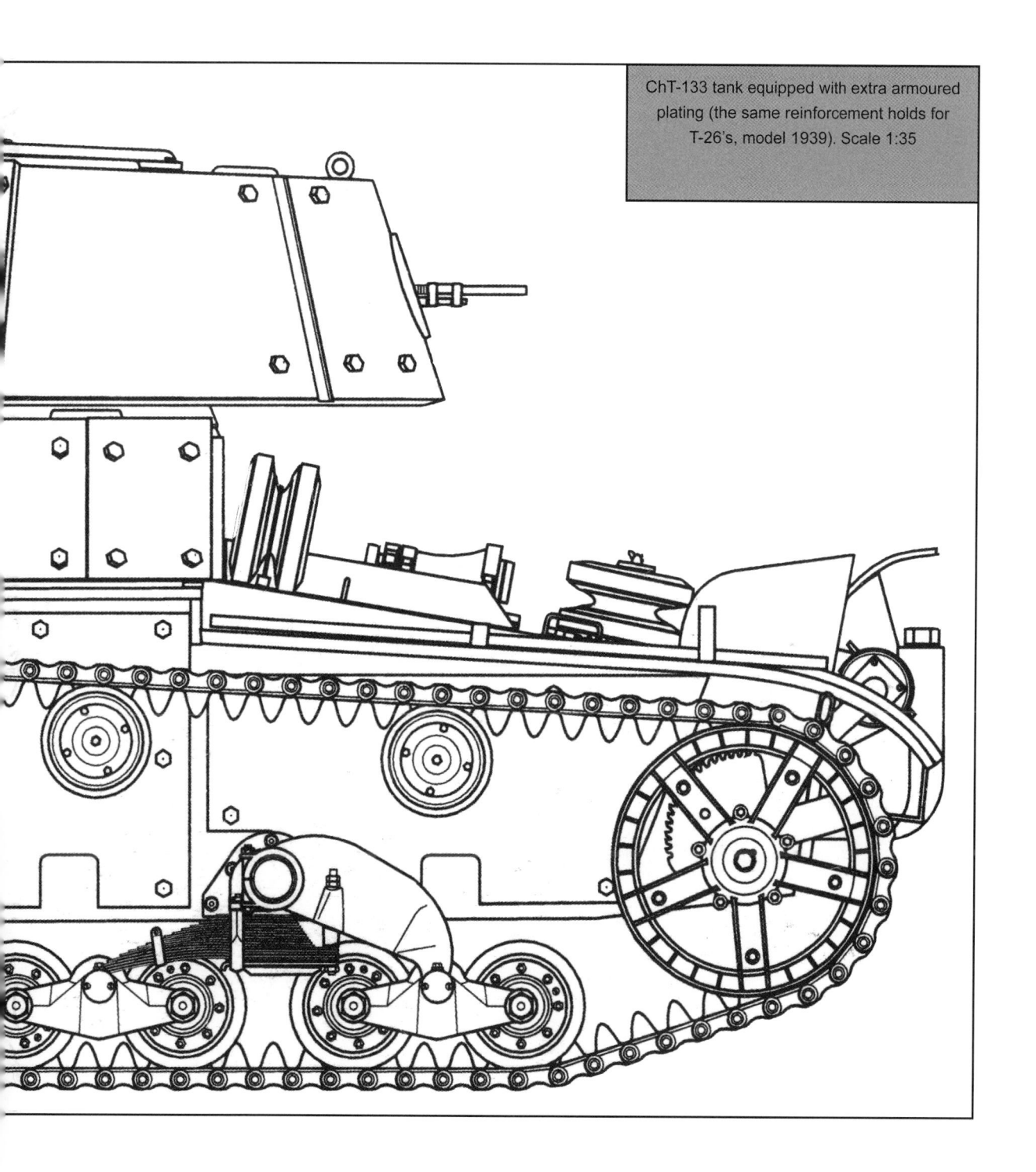

ChT-133 tank equipped with extra armoured plating (the same reinforcement holds for T-26's, model 1939). Scale 1:35

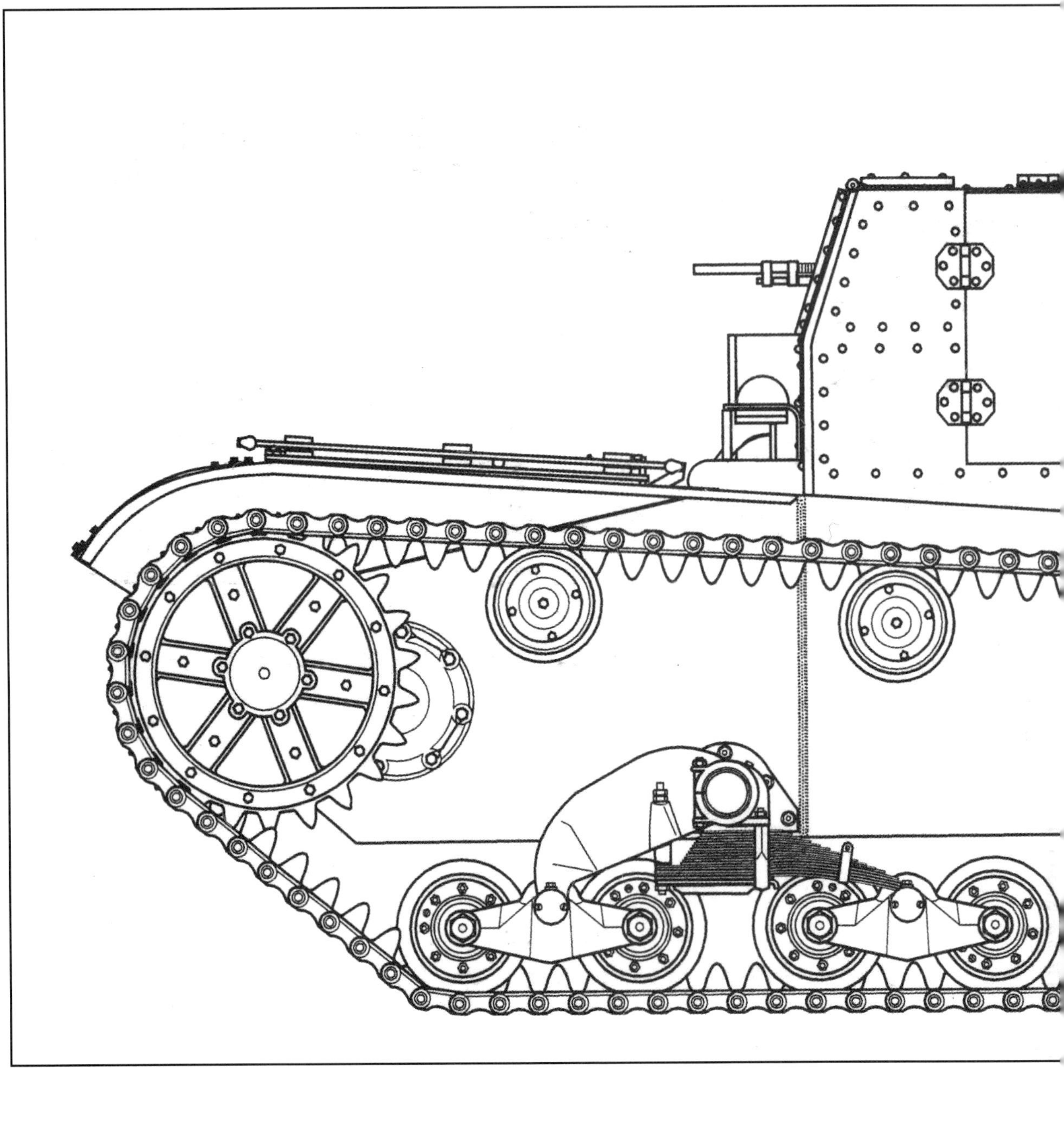

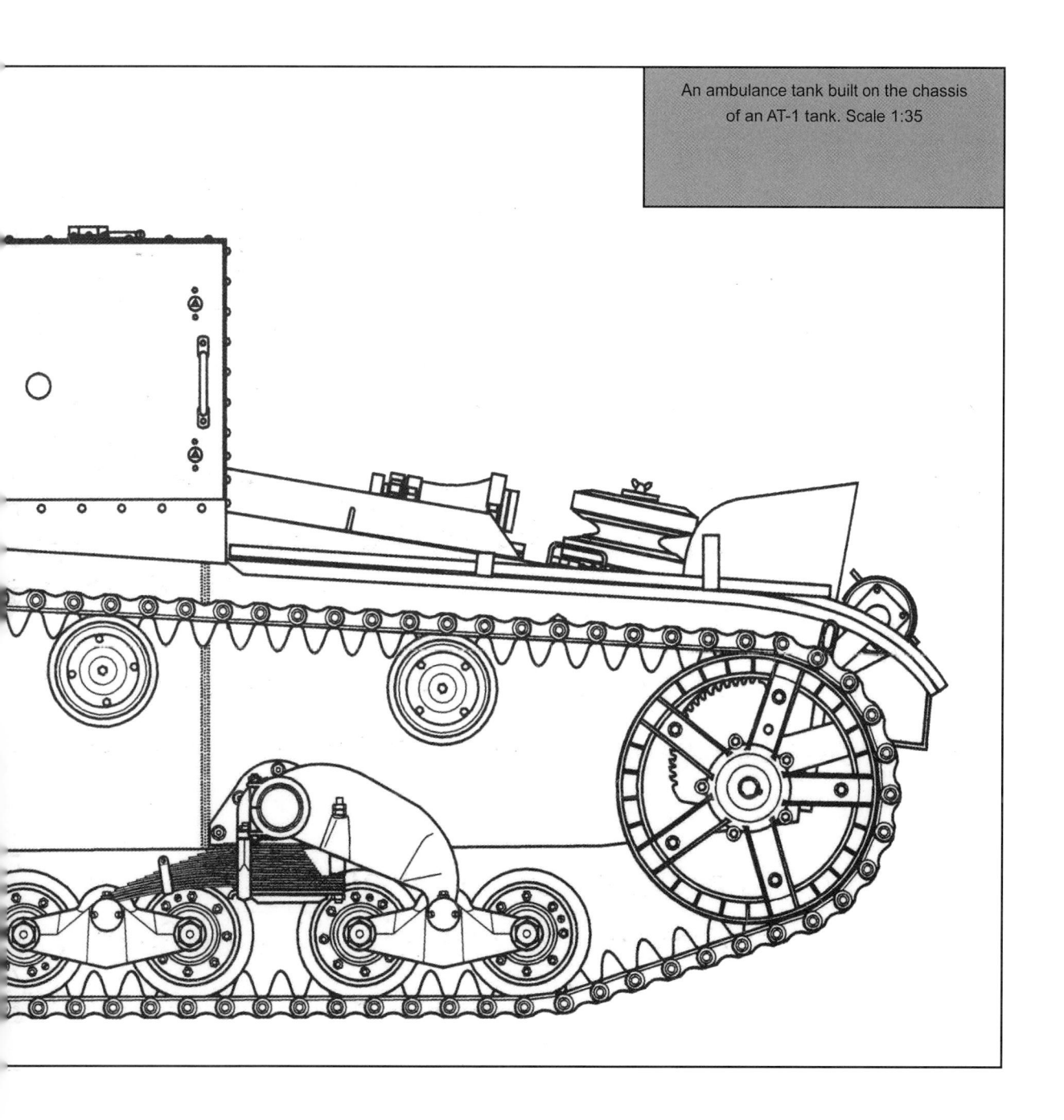

An ambulance tank built on the chassis of an AT-1 tank. Scale 1:35

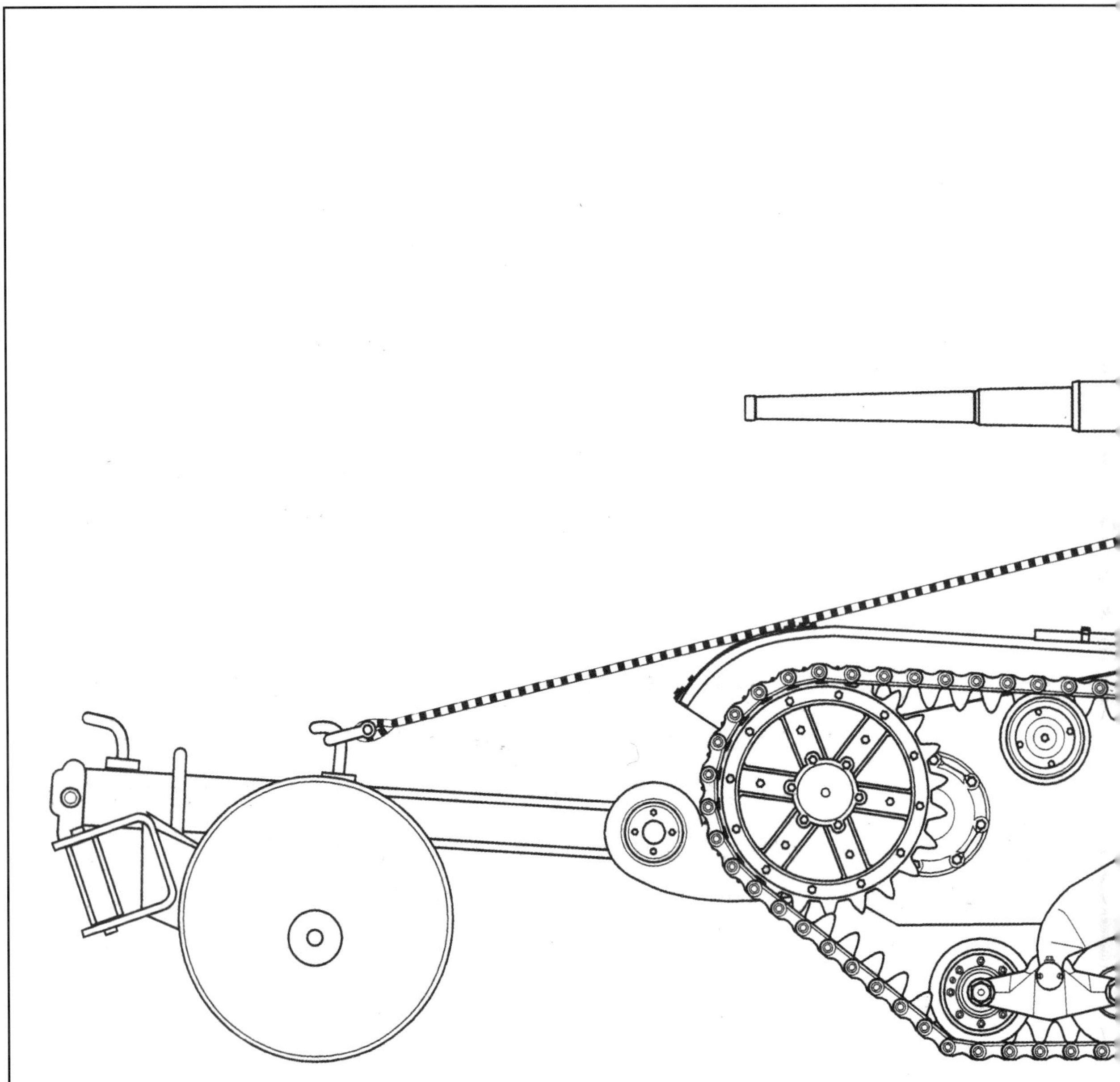

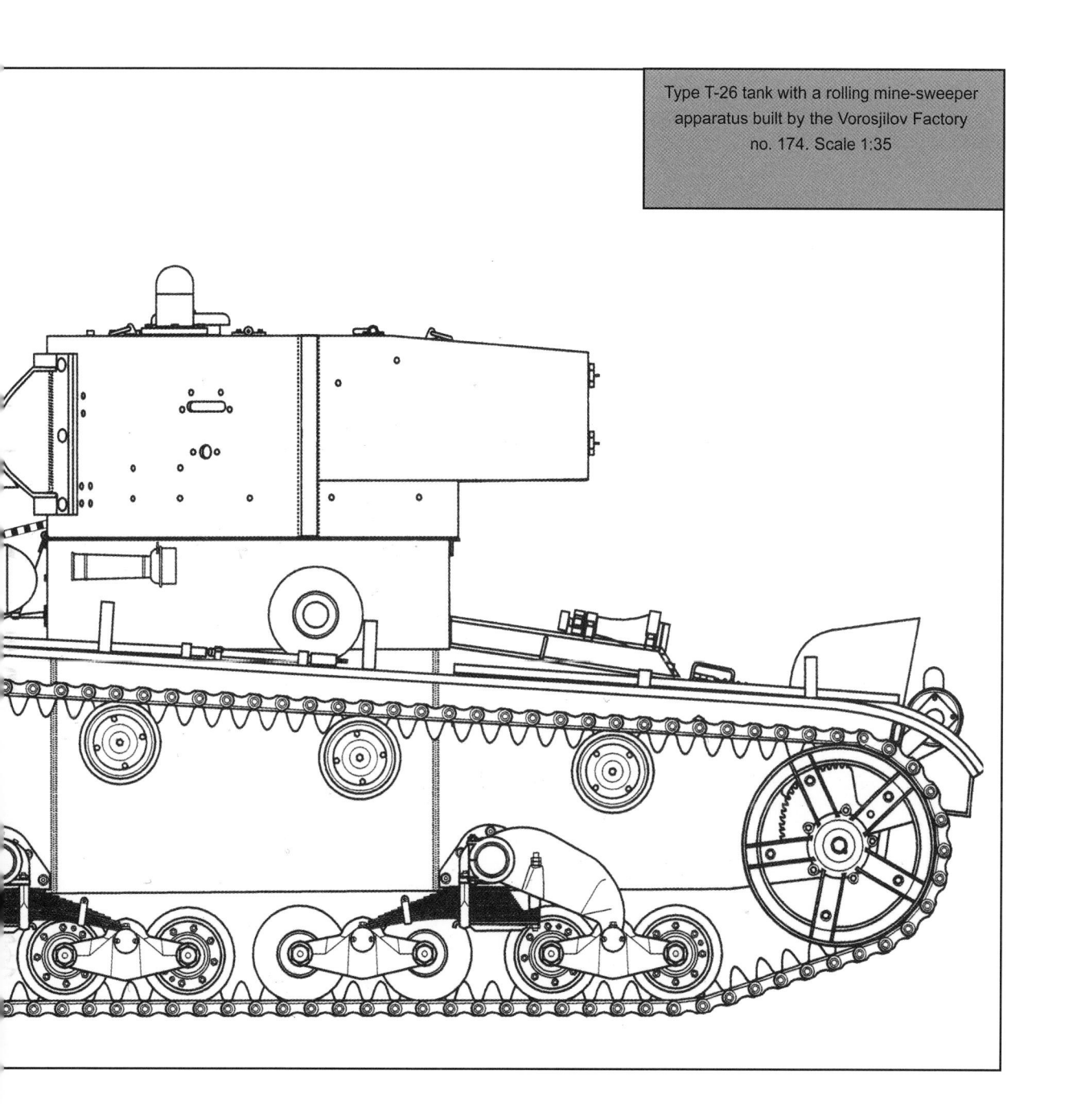

Type T-26 tank with a rolling mine-sweeper apparatus built by the Vorosjilov Factory no. 174. Scale 1:35

216

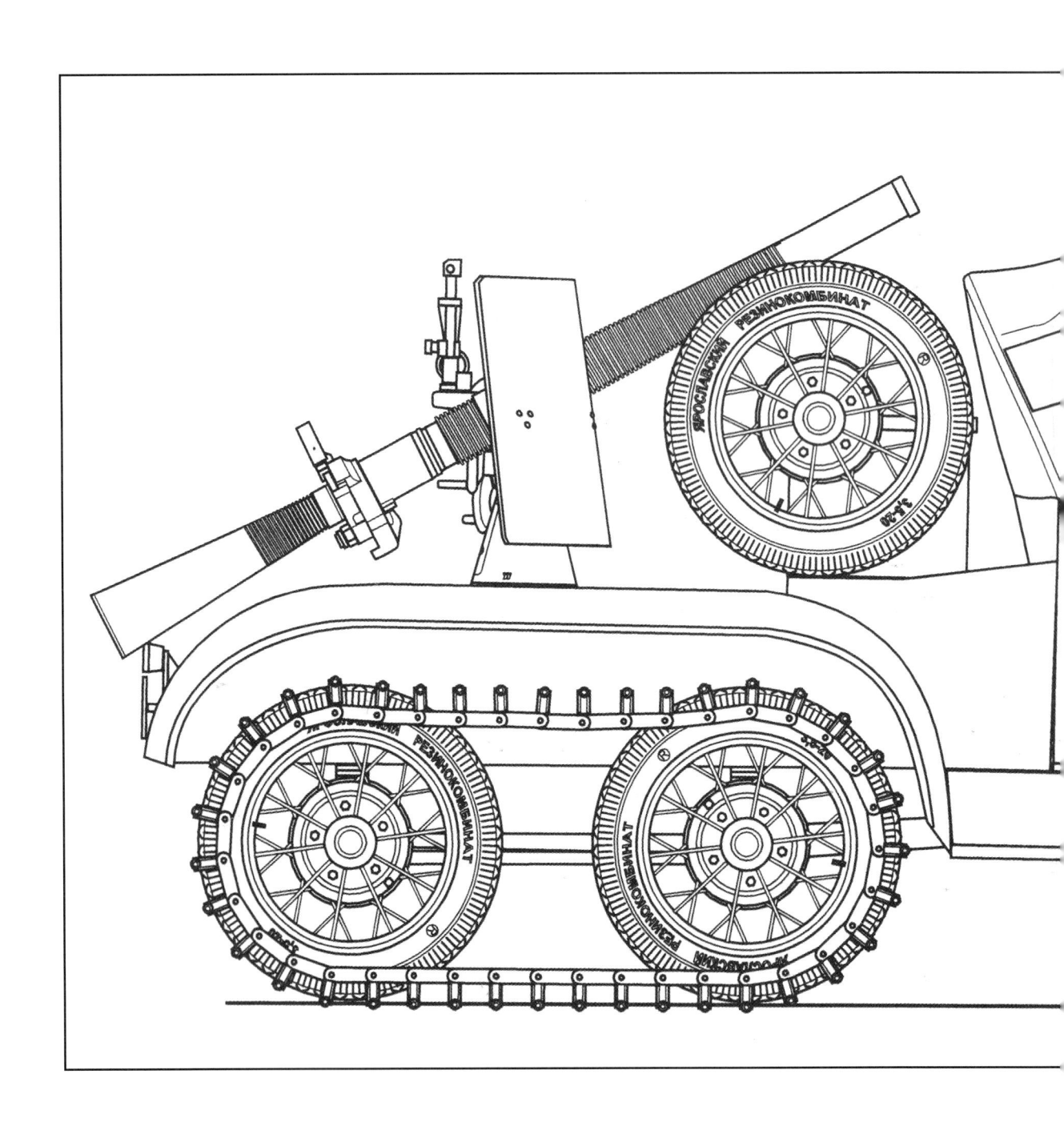

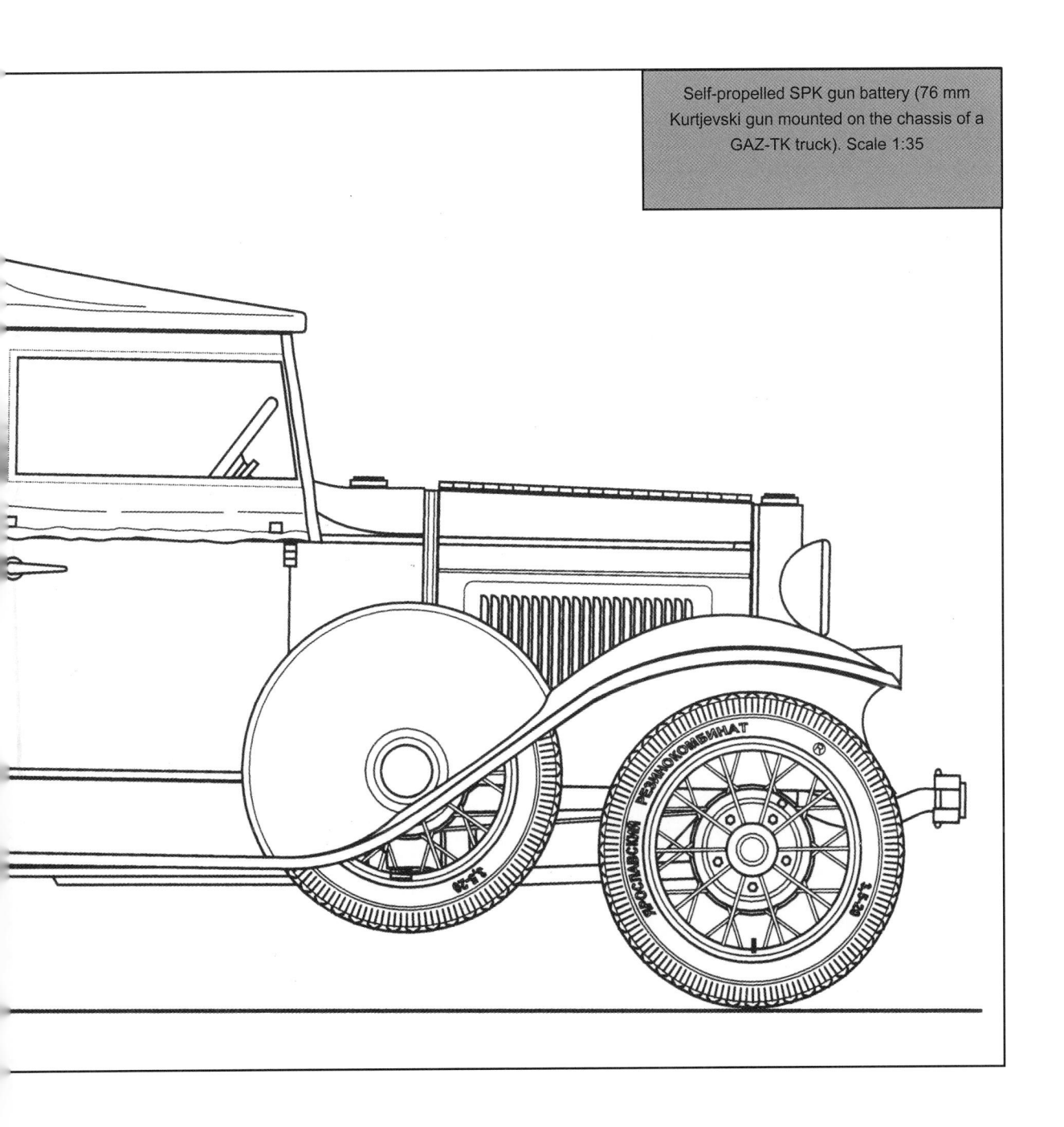

Self-propelled SPK gun battery (76 mm Kurtjevski gun mounted on the chassis of a GAZ-TK truck). Scale 1:35

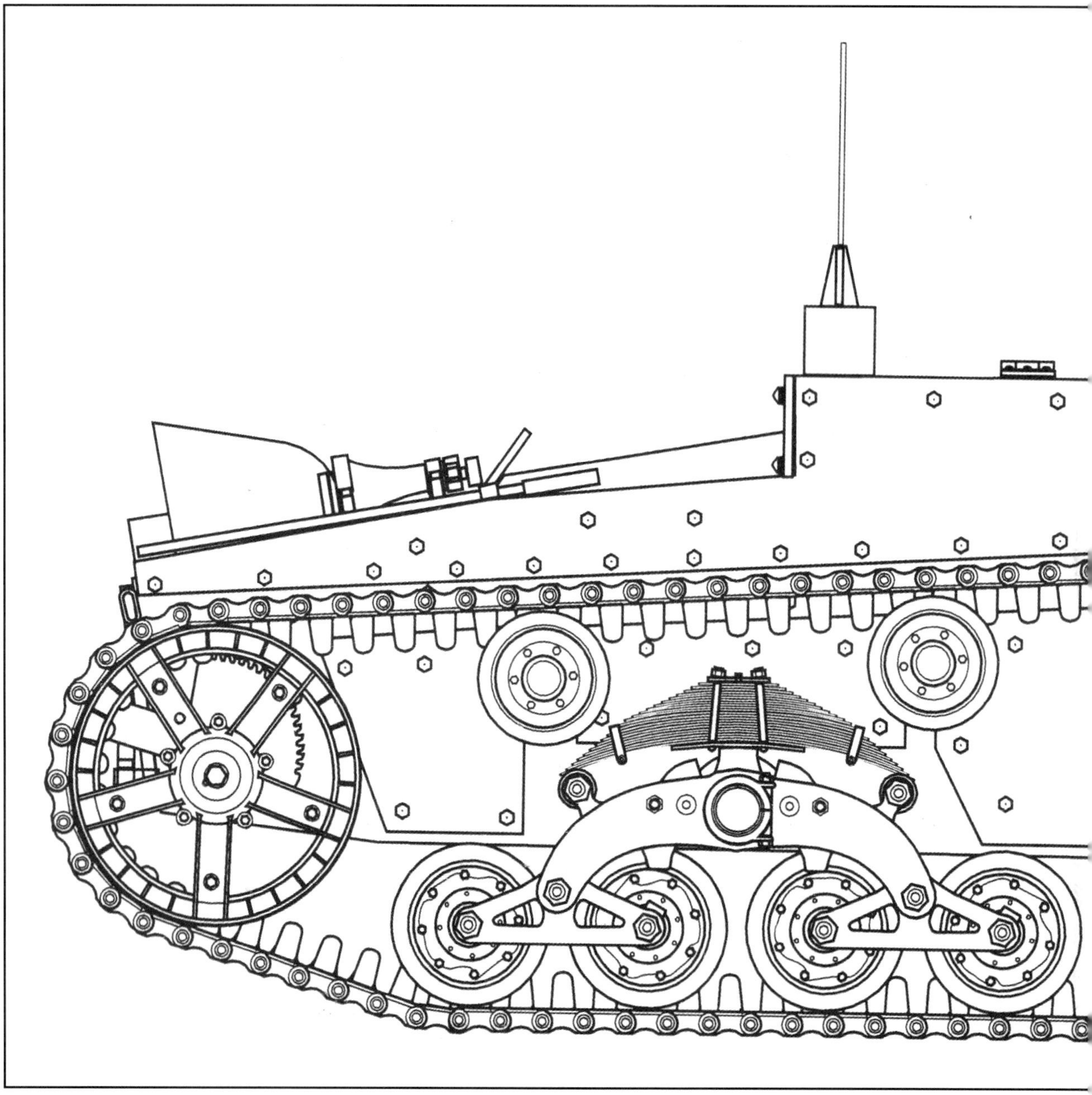

The radio-controlled tank

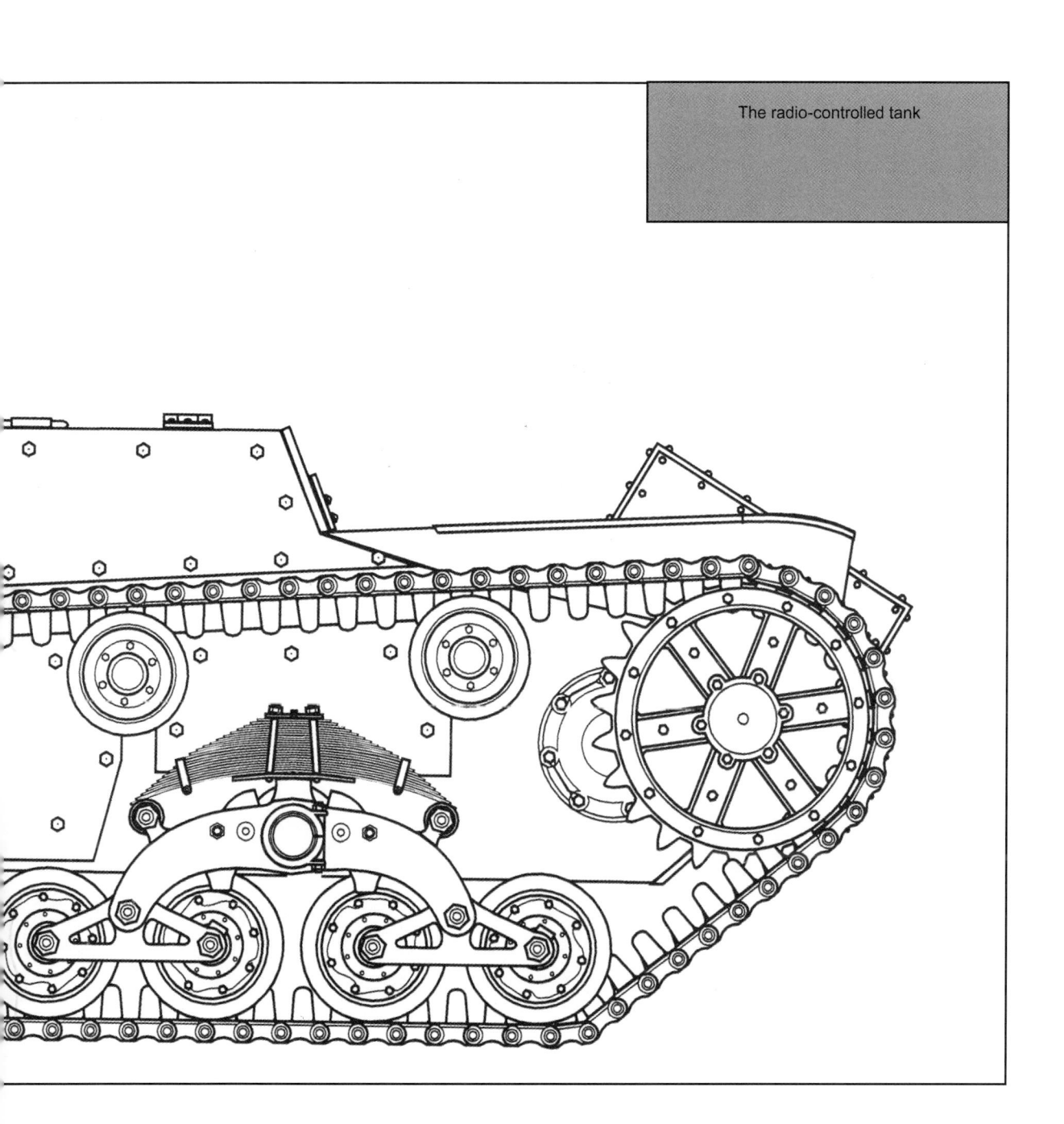

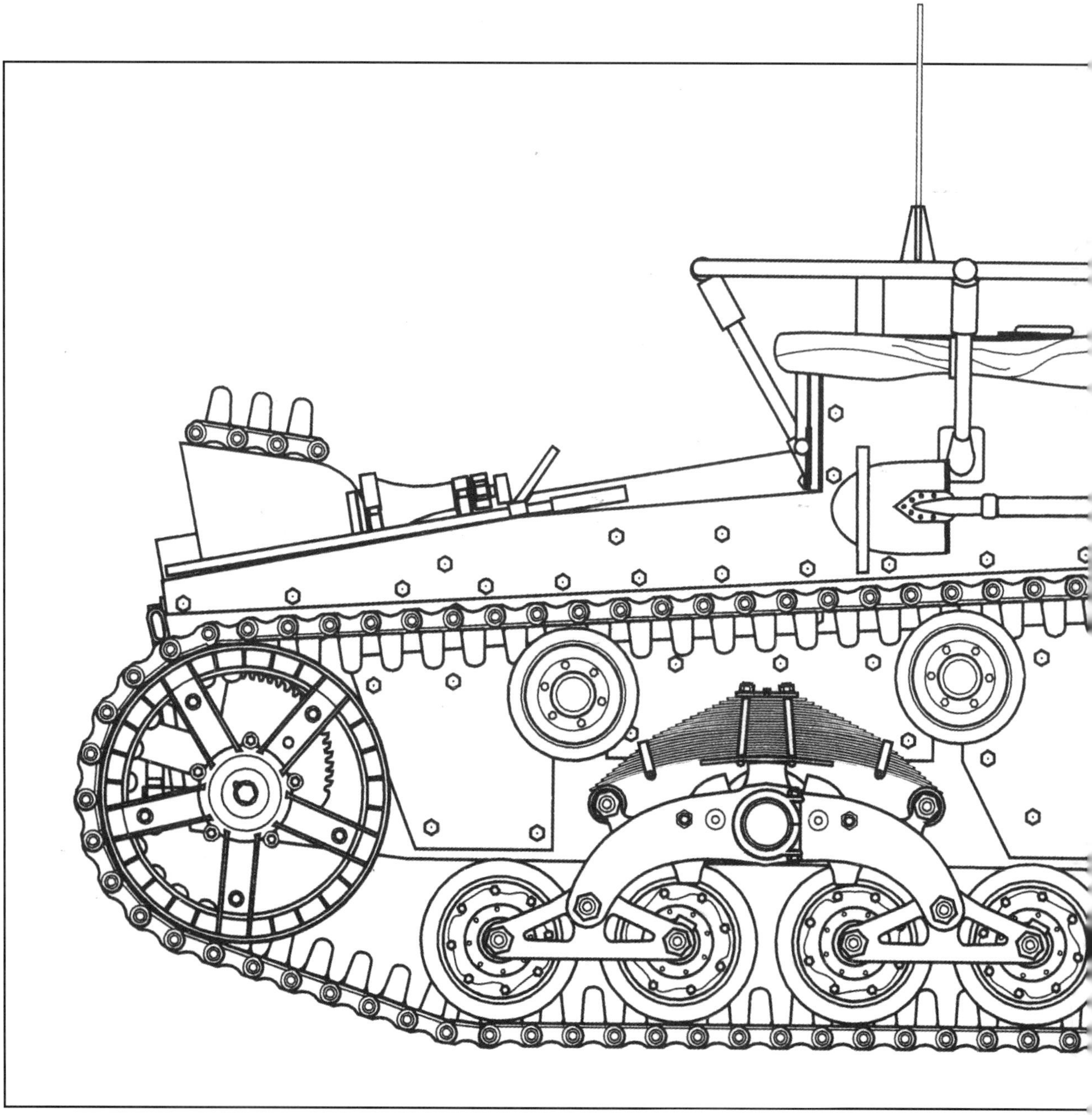

The leading/controlling tank

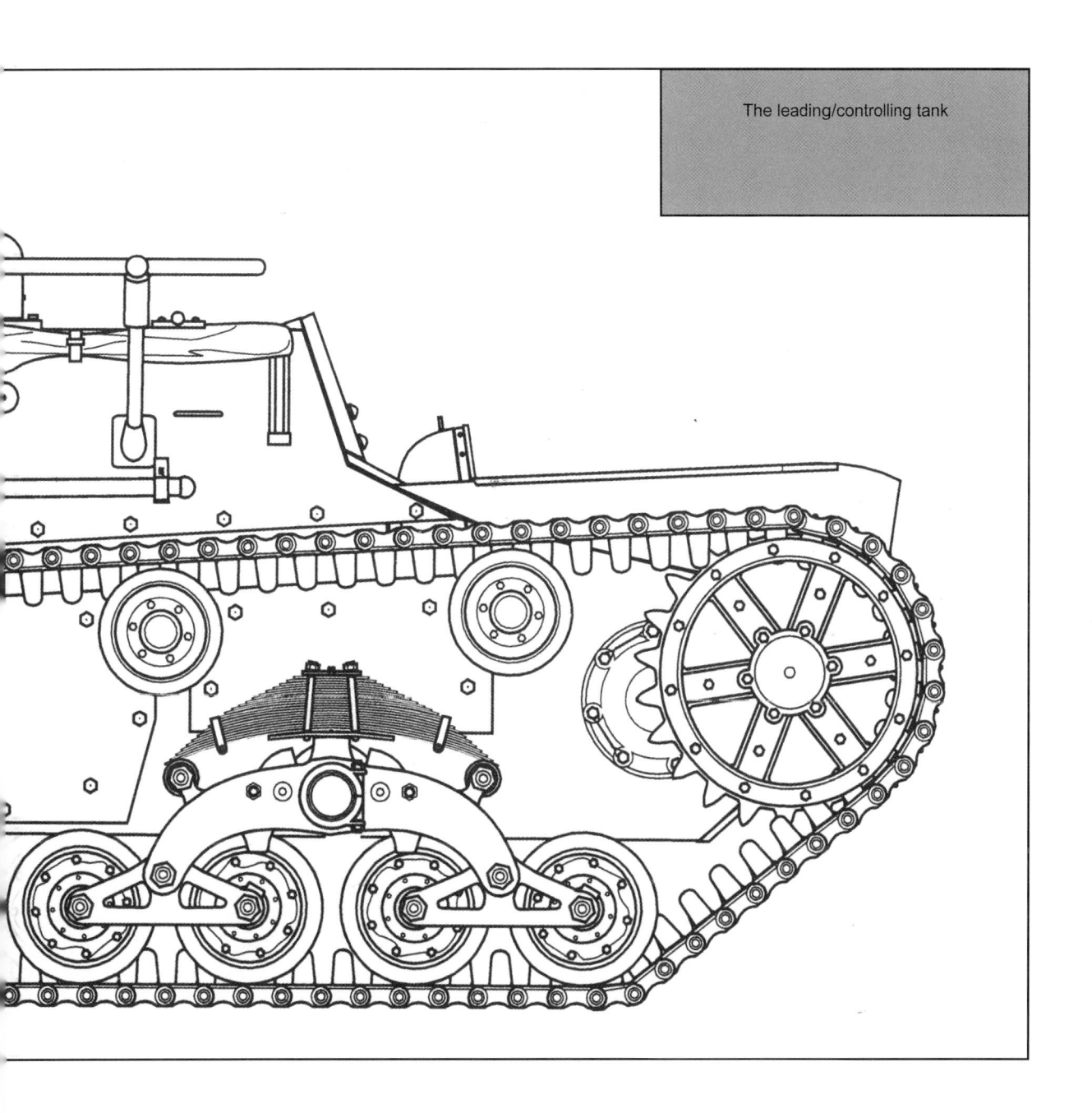